UNHAPPY FAMILIES

Clinical and Research Perspectives
on
Family Violence

Eli H. Newberger, M.D.
Assistant Professor of Pediatrics
Harvard Medical School
Director, Family Development Study
Children's Hospital, Boston

Richard Bourne, Ph.D., J.D.
Associate Professor of Sociology
Northeastern University
Attorney, Office of General Counsel
Children's Hospital, Boston

PSG PUBLISHING COMPANY, INC.
LITTLETON, MASSACHUSETTS

Library of Congress Cataloging in Publication Data
Main entry under title:

Unhappy families.

Includes index.
1. Family violence — United States — Addresses, essays, lectures. 2. Child abuse — United States — Addresses, essays, lectures. 3. Child molesting — United States — Addresses, essays, lectures. I. Newberger, Eli H. II. Bourne, Richard. [DNLM: 1. Family. 2. Violence. HQ 809 U57]
HQ809.3.U5U5 1985   362.8'2   85-3573
ISBN 0-88416-504-3 (pbk.)

Published by:
PSG PUBLISHING COMPANY, INC.
545 Great Road
Littleton, Massachusetts 01460

Printed in the United States of America

International Standard Book Number: 0-88416-504-3

Library of Congress Catalog Card Number: 85-3573

Last digit is the print number: 9 8 7 6 5 4 3

Happy families are all alike;
every unhappy family is
unhappy in its own way.

TOLSTOY, *Anna Karenina*

CONTRIBUTORS

Denise Bienfang, M.S.W.
Clinical Social Worker
Boston, Massachusetts

Richard Bourne, Ph.D., J.D.
Associate Professor of
  Sociology
Northeastern University
Attorney, Office of General
  Counsel
Children's Hospital
Boston, Massachusetts

Jessica H. Daniel, Ph.D.
Clinical Psychologist
Judge Baker Guidance Center
Boston, Massachusetts

Melvin Delgado, Ph.D.
Associate Professor, School of
  Social Work
Boston University
Boston, Massachusetts

William H. Dietz, M.D., Ph.D.
Assistant Professor of
  Pediatrics
Tufts University School of
  Medicine
Director, Clinical Nutrition
Division of Gastroenterology
  and Nutrition
Department of Pediatrics
New England Medical Center
Boston, Massachusetts

Michael Feldberg, Ph.D.
Lecturer in Criminal Justice
Boston University
Northeastern University
Boston, Massachusetts

David Finkelhor, Ph.D.
Associate Professor of
  Sociology
University of New Hampshire
Co-Director, Family Research
  Laboratory
Durham, New Hampshire

Richard J. Gelles, Ph.D.
Professor of Sociology
Dean of College of Arts and
  Science
University of Rhode Island
Kingston, Rhode Island

David G. Gil, D.S.W.
Professor of Social Policy
Director, Center for Social
  Change, Practice, and Theory
Heller Graduate School
Brandeis University
Waltham, Massachusetts

Gretchen Graef, M.S.W.
Co-Director, Sexual Abuse
  Treatment Team
Department of Psychiatry
Children's Hospital
Boston, Massachusetts

Linda Gudas, R.N., P.N.P.
Doctoral Candidate in Child
  Development
Tufts University
Medford, Massachusetts
Pediatric Nurse Practitioner
Children's Hospital
Boston, Massachusetts

Daniel B. Kessler, M.D.
Chief, Division of Child
  Development
Assistant Professor of
  Pediatrics
Cornell University Medical
  College
Assistant Attending Pediatrician
The New York Hospital
New York, New York

Jack Levin, Ph.D.
Professor of Sociology
Northeastern University
Boston, Massachusetts

Paul Mones, J.D.
Legal Director, Public Justice
  Foundation
Santa Monica, California

Carolyn Moore Newberger, Ed.D.
Clinical and Developmental
  Psychologist
Children's Hospital/Judge
  Baker Guidance Center
Boston, Massachusetts

Eli H. Newberger, M.D.
Assistant Professor of
  Pediatrics
Harvard Medical School
Director, Family Development
  Study
Children's Hospital
Boston, Massachusetts

Herschel D. Rosenzweig, M.D.
Adjunct Associate Professor of
  Psychiatry
University of Arizona
Director of Youth Services
Southern Arizona Mental
  Health Center
Director of Youth Services
Palo Verde Hospital
Tucson, Arizona

Beverly Weaver, R.N., C.S.
Partner, Beacon Associates
Brookline, Massachusetts

CONTENTS

PREFACE

The first sentence of *Anna Karenina* sends an enigmatic message to all concerned with family violence. "Happy families are all alike; every unhappy family is unhappy in its own way."

Families of victims of child abuse, child sexual abuse, and family violence all look alike to many professionals and public officials. This is due both to the biased case reporting process which favors poor families for identification and study, and to the superficial nature of practice in agencies where the task of protecting the victim is focused on a single decision point: whether to separate him or her from contact with kin.

The myth that family violence occurs only among the poor is dispelled somewhat by the few surveys of the prevalence of violence which avoid case reporting artifacts by selecting representative samples and asking individuals about their own experiences and practices. In our work at Children's Hospital, we have a continuing opportunity to observe how professionals assemble their knowledge and diagnostic formulations of childhood injuries and what they do about them. Our observations, and several studies, suggest that with regard to the problem of child abuse, class and race, as much as clinical severity, define who is identified as the victim.

That the myth persists indicates that it has some meaning. With respect to "child abuse," we believe the meaning is found in the way child abuse as a homogeneous entity functions to maintain our social equilibrium. Sociologist Richard Gelles, one of the contributors to this book, suggests that because we can point to the bad parents over there, what we do in our homes is OK. Professor David Gil, another contributor, carries the smokescreen metaphor a step further. The sensational nature of the child abuse problem, he argues, allows us as a society to ignore the fundamental needs of millions of our young, for food, housing, education, and health. We want and need "abusive families" to look alike, just so long as they are different from the rest of us.

The objective of this book is to provide straightforward and clear discussions of current practice and research on family violence in ways which will illuminate the many problems which we see in clinical work. Originally, these chapters were presented at interdisciplinary seminars for clinicians and researchers as a part of our Hospital's training program on family violence which is supported by research training grants from the Center for Studies of Violent and Antisocial Behavior of the National Institute of Mental Health and from the National Center on Child Abuse and Neglect in the Federal Department of Health and Human Services.

We and the contributors have edited the chapters in such a way as to weed out unnecessary scientific and clinical jargon and to preserve the conversational tone. We have kept some questions and responses which probe particular issues and which serve to illustrate the diverse perspectives brought to bear on the subject by professionals from many disciplines.

Our hope is that this book will enable the reader to see each unhappy family as different and worthy of being treated respectfully and well.

Family violence is an issue which commands attention from all of us, and no one person can sufficiently well understand or help a victim and his or her unhappy family. We depend ourselves on our cherished associates whose personal and professional commitments to unhappy families make our work possible. The establishment of the training program and seminar series which led to this book was a substantial additional effort on behalf of our co-workers, and we thank them here knowing that simply listing their names does not do justice to the long hours, sleepless nights, and struggles to sustain communication in the face of the interpersonal and interprofessional conflicts which go with the territory when one works on family violence. These colleagues are Jessica Daniel, Barbara Danzell, Howard Dubowitz, Debbie Fenn, Robert Hampton, Drew Hopping, Sylvia Krakow, Joanne Michalek, Stephen Shirk, Betty Singer, Pamela Whitney, and Ellen Weiss. We are indebted to Marilyn Felt whose expert editorial work helped to keep in focus the most important issues in the text. Our wives, Carolyn Moore Newberger and Carole Rice Bourne are pillars of strength and patience without whose love and support we could not continue to carry forth in this unhappy field of work.

Eli H. Newberger, M.D.
Richard Bourne, Ph.D., J.D.
Boston, Massachusetts
January 16, 1985

CHAPTER 1

Family Violence:
What We Know and Can Do

Richard J. Gelles

It is important that clinicians and researchers understand that detrimental interactions within families are of many types. They may differ in kind, in impact, in cause, and in treatment and policy. For the sake of convenience, however, they have all been compressed by professionals and the media into the generic term, *abuse*. So we have child abuse, wife abuse, elderly abuse, and parent abuse. The word *abuse* has become a political concept which stands for things that are done to family members which are thought by many to be harmful and about which people want to take some kind of remedial or ameliorative action. Placing things like the physical beating of children, the emotional neglect of children, and the failure to thrive syndrome under the term *child abuse* is convenient for communication but inconvenient and misleading for both research and clinical practice. While neglect may be related to child abuse, and while sexual abuse may be related to physical abuse, they are distinctive phenomenon arising from different causes and often requiring different intervention and preventive strategies.

My concern as a researcher has been exclusively with physical violence between family members ranging from the normal kind of violence such as spanking, which is typically dismissed by clinicians as being part of family relations, up to lethal forms of family violence (for example, homicide), about which there is consensus that they are inappropriate in family relations. That is not to say that neglect, emotional abuse, or verbal abuse are not problematic and harmful, but to say that the act of physically striking another human being is conceptually and programmatically distinct from acts of omission.

FREQUENCY OF FAMILY VIOLENCE

The estimated incidence of family violence, child abuse, wife abuse, husband abuse, and elderly beating, varies on who is asked. It varies because of the variable and frequently imprecise definitions used and because most people base their estimates of incidence on cases that come to public attention. In the state of Rhode Island in 1967, officially there were not any cases of child abuse. By 1977, it was in excess of 1500 cases, leading many people in that state to believe there was an epidemic. What was ignored were two social forces: one was the passage of a mandatory reporting law, and the second was an increased sensitivity on the part of clinicians that injuries to children may be inflicted by their parents.

Another problem with official statistics on child abuse and neglect is that they are skewed. Only certain injuries which occur to certain types of people in certain types of families are officially designated as abuse. Poor families, black families, non-English speaking families, and socially marginal families are disproportionately susceptible to having the label *abuse* attached to behavior in their households. Mainstream families, well-to-do families, and families of physicians, attorneys, and college professors find that injuries to their children are almost uniformly classified as accidents.

In order to correct this bias, in 1976 we carried out a study most people said could not be done. Believing that the studying of officially reported or clinical cases of child and wife abuse was not an accurate way of finding out how extensive family violence was, we interviewed a representative sample of 2143 American families. We knew that we could not march into the American household and ask if they had stopped beating their child, wife, or parents, so we used an instrument called the Conflict Tactics Scales. The scale begins by introducing the idea that all families have conflict between one another and typically use many ways of dealing with this conflict. We then read a list of some 20 items and asked if the subjects had used these techniques to deal with conflict and how frequently.

The first technique was, "We discuss the issue calmly." By item 16, we were asking respondents whether they slapped or spanked, and the last item on the list was how often they used a knife or a gun. The answers we got to the latter question amazed us. From the responses we could project that approximately 50,000 parents will use knives or guns against their children each year. Nearly half a million American parents have used knives or guns against their children while raising them; 175,000 siblings used a knife or a gun against a sibling in the previous year. And some 100,000 husbands and wives use guns and knives against one another in one year. That is not nearly as amazing as the fact that people reported these behaviors to us. It may be assumed that when people tell us that they used a knife or a gun against their child, they are not necessarily thinking that it is terribly wrong.

We combined the items we saw as abusive and violent to try to get a handle on how extensive the problem of child abuse and wife abuse is in the United States. We included kicking, biting, punching, hitting or trying to hit with an object, beating, threatening with a gun or a knife, or using a gun or a knife. For women, our estimate is 3.8% of women living with men (either married to those men or living together in a family-like relationship) are abused each year (with a sampling error of ± 1%). Child abuse involves 3.6% or 1.6 million children aged 3 to 17. That figure would go up if we included children under age 3 (we did not because of the nature of the study) and if we included single parent families (we did not because we also wanted to study spouse abuse). Consequently, one could realistically think about children at a rate of 4% or 2 million rather than 3.6% or 1.6 million. The figure for parents who are struck by their children, including only acts that could do harm (acts of children over 11 years old), is about 3.5%, between 500,000 and 1 million parents.

Considerable newsprint has been devoted to elderly abuse this year out of proportion to how much research has been done. Estimates are, however, that growing old does not insulate a person from family violence and that people over 65 who have frequent contact with their children also run a risk of abuse at approximately the same rate as other family relationships, between 3% and 4%.

For a clinician or a physician in practice, the percent figures and the million figures probably do not hold a lot of meaning. If abused people were distributed across the population evenly, which they are not, clinicians would then be seeing abused children at a rate of 1/22 children seen, and they would be seeing abused wives at a rate of 1/21 wives seen. They would be seeing battered elderly (and this is low because we are dealing with people over 65 who are married, who had children, whose children are still alive, and who may see their children) at approximately a rate of 1/22 elderly persons seen.

Family violence is far more extensive than any official statistics have ever indicated, yet the figures are in all likelihood underestimates because they are based on what people are willing to tell an interviewer in a 60-minute interview. My guess is that each of the abuse figures is low by a factor of 20% to 50%.

Incidence data simply establish the nature of the problem and indicate how much concrete economic and social resources have to be brought to bear. If categories of victims are added up, it is evident that this problem affects some 8 to 10 million American families of the 56 million in the United States.

Labeling Bias

After determining incidence, the second question is, in which families are these violent events most likely to occur and why? This is where I want to discuss definitions and labeling. Two modes of research most frequently used by family violence researchers are: 1) drawing cases of abuse from the local protective service agency; or 2) if that agency happens to be particularly nasty toward researchers, which is sometimes the case, making a friend with a mental health agency or a hospital such as Children's Hospital and drawing cases from their clinical case load, and then finding some kind of matched comparison group and drawing conclusions and analysis.

There is a distinct problem in these research modes, and it was made clear in a study of 76 pediatricians in Baltimore, Maryland. The pediatricians were presented with a contrived medical file which had all of the normal social and medical information about a child's family. They were presented with a medical file and asked to review the information in it, and to assess an injury that had occurred to the young child in the medical record. They were then asked if they thought this injury is child abuse, how severe it is, and whether they would report it to the authorities in the state of Maryland. What the physicians did not know was that one factor was manipulated in the medical record. Half the physicians received a file in which the child's father was identified as a truck driver. The other half got a child whose father was identified as a salesman. Everything else including the injury, the x-rays, and social information was identical. The son of the truck driver was 40% more likely to be reported as a case of child abuse than the son of the salesman. In the second administration, another single factor was varied, and that was the race of the child. Occupations were the same. Everything was the same in both files only one child was described as black, and one child was described as white. The black injured child was 33% more likely to be reported as abused than the white injured child.

If one then bases research conclusions on an analysis of cases of child abuse diagnosed by physicians, then one would conclude that manual laborers and blacks have higher rates of child abuse when, in fact, being a manual laborer or being black contributes to getting caught as much as it does to who actually carries out the act.

Correlation with Family Violence

In the early discussions of family violence as well as in current discussions, we employed a "kind-of-person" model, to try to explain which people abuse children and which children would be abused. The "person model" is still in favor. It is in favor because people who make diagnoses are trained epidemiologically to look at kinds of people; physicians, psychiatrists, and social welfare personnel are trained to look at individuals and find differences between individuals. The "kind-of-person" model reached its highest point of absurdity when an author wrote in a prominent medical journal that parents who abuse their children were characterized by an inability to control their aggressions, and thereby the personality trait of inability to control aggressions should be looked for in diagnosing child abuse. As in this case, it has happened frequently that the proposed cause of child abuse has, in fact, been a synonym for the words child abuse.

It is generally agreed now that, at most, 10% of wife abuse and child abuse cases are attributable to mental illness and character disorders or, in other words, to "kinds of people." The other 90% of the abusers defy clinical classification as suffering from individual aberrations. They are not different psychologically from most people.

Generally four factors are found to be related to family violence. Note, "found to be related," should be understood as a probability statement, not a determining statement. The first factor is that family violence is, in many cases, transmitted intergenerationally. An abused child's chances of becoming an abusive adult are, in some instances, a thousand times greater than a nonabused child. However, the base rate of child abuse is not especially high, 3.6%; so a thousand times greater does not mean that every abused child grows up to be an abusive parent. In terms of my own research findings, there is only about a 50% chance that an abused child will become an abusive parent. For a social scientist, that is a strong association. For a clinician, that is too weak to base a prediction on. It is important for clinicians to realize that although the social scientists jump for joy over strong associations, strong associations do not necessarily make predictive instruments.

The second factor is that abuse of all kinds is more likely to occur in lower socioeconomic families. Families below the poverty line have rates of wife and child abuse which exceed the rates of those making $25,000 or more per year by a factor of two. But again, all poor people are not abusers, and abuse can be found in some fairly well-to-do families.

The third factor is that abusive families of all kinds are characterized by significant social isolation which can be identified by noticing how few organizations in the community abusive families belong to, how little contact they have with neighbors and relatives and families, and how many moves they make. Abusive families typically do not live in the same neighborhood for a long time. One of the factors that we have found very strongly related was living in a house in a neighborhood less than two years.

The fourth factor is social stress. The higher the social stress the greater the chance that the family will be abusive.

With regard to other factors related to family violence, blacks and whites show no difference in rates of child abuse. That should not have been the case on two grounds. One, the reported cases are so disproportionately black that we were led to believe that blacks were more abusive than whites. Also, on a national scale, blacks make less money, have less education, and have poorer jobs. By and large the black sample we surveyed corresponded to blacks in our society, and yet despite their low income and high stress, they were not more abusive. The explanation for this was that our study showed that blacks, compared to whites, had more contact with relatives, more community membership, and more contact with the church. They were able to network both on a community and a relationship basis to ameliorate the stress that might have led to child abuse. This same networking, however, did not ameliorate the chances of wife abuse, and the rates in the black community were considerably higher than rates among whites.

Some Other Data of Interest

Agnostics and atheists have higher rates of abuse. Another factor is that abuse is more likely to happen in young families than in older ones. Since violence is more likely to be found in young people, and younger marriages have more transitions, that finding makes a good deal of sense. Education did not prove to be the factor we thought it would; low education was not related. Income, as I said, was related. Manual workers do have higher rates of abuse than white collar workers, and part-time and unemployed workers had higher rates of family violence than men who were employed full-time, with the rate for the few part-time workers being double the rate for husbands with full-time jobs. The last factor is the power structure of households. If a family moves toward sharing decisions and an egalitarian household, the chances of violence taking place may possibly be reduced by half.

CAUSATION

Causal explanations are few to be found. People abuse family members because they can. There are rewards to be gained from being abusive: the immediate reward of getting someone to stop doing something; of inflicting pain on someone as revenge; of controlling behavior; or of having power. All of these rewards are evident in other social settings. Why don't people beat up their neighbors when they return the lawn mower broken? Why don't people beat up their boss, when he makes them stay late on the night they have show tickets which cannot be returned? Why don't people beat up their annoying co-workers? The motivation is there and is, perhaps, as strong as the motivation in families. They do not because the costs are too high. Beating up a boss could result in being kicked back, fired or having the police called. The police are known to respond faster when people are beating up a stranger than when they are beating up a family member. Beat up a stranger and the result could be assault charges or incarceration. Very few of those controls operate in families. A person does not lose his job for beating his wife or beating his children. The risk of official social control is rarely run; judges are despondent when faced with a choice of leaving a family intact or criminally prosecuting the abuser. The tradition in families is for a more powerful person to beat on someone less powerful, someone who cannot return and inflict even physical costs.

From my point of view, exchange theory and social control theory are the explanations. In a therapeutic setting, the abuser might say to the therapist: "I really like my kids, I really feel guilty, I feel terrible about it, but they got me so mad, I could not help myself," or, "I drank so much, I could not control myself," or, "Wouldn't you do that if you had such and such happen to you?" If a therapist buys in on the theory that kids can be so maddening, that alcohol makes a person so loose, that wives can nag so much that a person cannot control himself, that therapist licenses that person to abuse again. Anytime a clinician buys in on these rationalizations, or agrees that he would do the same thing under that stress, he takes away the costs that should have impact on the internal social control of the abuser.

CLINICAL INTERVENTION AND SOCIAL POLICY

That statement begins a rather brief discussion of how we apply knowledge to clinical practice. Very briefly, very generally, from the point of view of diagnosis it is important not to be ruled by single factor explanations. Nor is the intergenerational transmission of abusiveness so strong that a positive diagnosis can be made from that information alone.

Child abuse is not a pathology in the medical sense, and it is not amenable to either a germ explanation or diagnosis. Full medical, psychological and sociological information is required in order to diagnose how an injury occurred and whether it was accidental or inflicted.

From the point of view of treatment, I cannot say that I am wedded to any particular modality. I do have a bias toward family treatment as opposed to individual treatment because the family system is what spawns the violence, not an attribute of the individual. The treatment goal and the most general way of presenting it is this: if the cause of family violence is that people abuse family members because they can, the goal of the clinician is to make it so they cannot.

A clinician should not accept, even if he believes them, the rationalization, "I cannot control myself, I drink too much, I've got an alcohol problem." He should not make such a rapport with the abuser that he minimizes the impact of what the abuser has done. The clinician must consider ways of raising the costs without damaging the self concept of the abuser and other family members. It does not do much good to spend numerous therapy sessions getting the abuser to not only accept responsibility for the act, but to accept the pejorative term child abuser. Instead, generating informal mechanisms of social control in that household should be emphasized, ie, getting somebody to play bystander or, at worst, policeman. Homemakers serve two wonderful functions: one, they alleviate stress and two, they are there, and people behave differently when a non-family member is present. How can we reduce the privacy in that household and increase the level of social control? How can we reduce the oligarchy of that household that allows husbands to beat their wives with impunity because the woman has no way of redressing the grievance? Can we change the decision making process?

In terms of social policy, the same issue is writ larger. Can we as a society decide that child abuse and wife abuse cause too much damage to be tolerated? Can we take steps to change the norms which say that it is all right to be violent toward family members? Can we make it so that people believe that people are not for hitting? Can we take a step that Sweden took and say that corporal punishment is improper in school and at home? Can we disarm the American family, conceding the point that criminals and presidential assassins will always get their hands on guns if they want them? Criminals and assassins account for only half of all homicides; the other half, our family members, destroy one another with handguns they have purchased to protect themselves from strangers. Lastly, can we help the family develop into an institution where there is equity, economic equity in terms of gender, and the ability to ameliorate stresses rather than generate them? Can we change the family from an institution that exceeds all but the military in the use of violence into an institution which assists children and parents in achieving their developmental potential?

BIBLIOGRAPHY

Finkelhor D, Gelles R, Hotaling G, Straus M: *The Dark Side of Families: Current Family Violence Research*. Beverly Hills, CA, Sage Publications, 1983.

Gelles RJ: *The Violent Home: A Study of Physical Aggression Between Husbands and Wives*. Beverly Hills, CA, Sage Publications, 1974.

Gelles RJ: The social construction of child abuse. *Am J Orthopsychiatry* 1975;45:363-371.

Gelles RJ: Methods for studying sensitive family topics. *Am J Orthopsychiatry* 1978;48:408-424.

Gelles RJ: Child abuse as psychopathology: a sociological critique and reformation. *Am J Orthopsychiatry* 1973;43:611-621.

Gelles RJ: Violence in the family: a review of research in the seventies. *J Marriage Family* 1980;42:873-885.

Gelles RJ: Applying research on family violence to clinical practice. *J Marriage Family* 1982;44:9-20.

Giovannoni JM, Becerra RM: *Defining Child Abuse*. New York, Free Press, 1979.

Hornung C, McCullough B, Sugimoto T: Status relationships in marriage: risk factors in spouse abuse. *J Marriage Family* 1981; 43:679-692.

Straus M, Gelles R, Steinmetz S: *Behind Closed Doors: Violence in the American Family*. Garden City, Anchor/Doubleday, 1980.

CHAPTER 2

The Political and Economic Context of Child Abuse

David G. Gil

We tend to think of violence in families as something separate from everything else in our daily lives, something that perhaps is rooted in people's personalities. This shuts us off from a possibility of unraveling the real dynamics and hence having a chance of reducing or preventing violence in people's homes. I should define what I mean by violence in the most general sense. To do this I have to start with the concept of human development. I assume — and I cannot say that I have evidence for it, nor is there evidence for the opposite — that development is an innate process in genetic material. It happens spontaneously provided organisms find themselves in environments from which they can derive the necessities of their existence. There is no need to push an organism to develop. When you put a seed into the ground and there is rain and sun and nutrients, it will become whatever it is capable of becoming. I think that human beings at birth or probably at conception are very capable and potentially rich beings, and they have the tendency of unfolding their potential provided the situation doesn't obstruct that process.

Violence, to me, is any human originated act or condition that obstructs the development process which would occur spontaneously. The obstruction can be a physical act, or it can be a negative quality of interactions that interferes with the developmental needs of the self. Finally, on a collective level, on the societal level, we create situations which inevitably result in obstacles to the development of people. Major illustrations of this are schools, many hospitals, and a variety of institutional arrangements, like poverty and slums, which obviously violate the conditions under which optimum development can take place. One has to differentiate between interpersonal violence in day to day interaction, and structural societal violence which is intrinsic to the arrangement of institutions, and by which a society arranges its overall way of life. They are different, but the important thing is that they are not apart from one another — they interact.

I submit that violence that takes place on the personal level is really a reaction to the violence to which people are exposed in the institutional and societal context. If at work I experience conditions that violate my developmental needs, then I absorb throughout the day this oppressive condition; when I get back into the private sphere of my home where I am not subject to the formal controls of the work place, the violence that I have absorbed all day long gets discharged. The family is the perfect setting for this kind of discharge. If we did not have it we would probably have to create it as a balance wheel against the violence of everyday life. One of the functions of the family is to reestablish balance for all of us whose emotional balance gets unsettled throughout the day. In the family we can discharge these feelings of stress and anger. That then becomes the interpersonal violence we are so concerned about.

This connection should not be accepted as true, but as one point of view and it should be tested out, examined through introspection, as we watch our own feelings in everyday life and our responses at home. If these assumptions are true, then domestic violence cannot be overcome in the home. It would have to be dealt with in the arena where our institutional and societal relations are determined, which is the political arena. My conclusion is that prevention of family violence requires a revolution in our way of life that would rearrange or redesign our modes of production and distribution in a manner that is conducive to the full development of every child and adult and aging person.

Structural Violence

To make some of this more concrete, I will talk primarily about aspects of *structural* violence, because the general public is familiar with aspects of *domestic* violence. If one wants to understand the dynamics of structural violence, one has to examine a number of interrelated domains of social existence. These domains include the way a society goes about providing itself with the necessities of existence. We have to look at how we deal with resources from which life is derived, how we deal with production and work, and what we do with the products of these efforts. We also have to look at our consciousness or ideology that gets us to act in certain ways which are not the only ways in which people can sustain existence. We will have to look at values because they are an important aspect of keeping a way of life the same.

What we do with the resources on which our existence depends is almost funny. We tend not to think about it, and that is why we do not change. We pile resources into big concentrations, and we also waste large quantities of resources. That may be an oversimplification, but we are using all the natural resources and the human created resources in a constant effort to acquire more under the control of fewer people. These are simply the dynamics of capitalism. Historically, this behavior led to a situation where most people do not own anything. Even knowledge, another very important resource of human life, is highly concentrated. Universities where we generate, store and transmit knowledge tend to exclude most people.

What do those who control resources do with them? Certainly they don't use them to meet everybody's needs. They use them to get control over more resources. This is called investment. They invest it in business and generating profit, which means gaining control over more resources. It is an irrational economic system which cuts off almost everybody from the possibility of working under one's own direction, because work means bringing together human capacities with aspects of the material world and earlier products. If these are separated from people, they cannot work at their initiative and own direction, but depend on the interests of others for the opportunity to become employed.

Nobody gets hired unless, directly or indirectly, he or she makes possible the further accumulation of resources for those who control the workplace. Work processes are designed not to enrich the life of the workers, but to enrich materially the ones who employ the workers. Work gets divided into meaningless fragments because some experts have figured out that it is more profitable if it is meaningless. About 90% of the work force will spend their work life in meaningless, repetitive routine activities under the control and direction and design not of themselves but of others. That is the typical situation of everyday work life.

Our way of life is inevitably violent toward most participants because it is oriented not toward the satisfaction of psychological and biological needs, but toward transforming humans into what economists call factors of production. If a person is a factor of production then he is not a human being. He is used in the calculations of those who control production as an attachment of their machines and computers, and he is experiencing an intense violation of his human essence throughout his waking hours. That violence results in indigestion in a psychological sense. Throwing up what has been digested is the violence we inflict on one another.

Human relations tend to be antagonistic in the context of profit seeking. Profit-making requires people who are willing to work for low wages. For people to work for low wages there has to be an abundance of workers compared to available jobs. We call this unemployment. Unemployment is an artifact of a particular way of organizing or distributing available work. Give too much to some and too little to others. Work could be distributed in other ways, but unemployment is necessary for cheap work. However, as soon as unemployment is a normal phenomenon, there is competition for everything related to work. In applying to medical school for instance, one prefers to be chosen and does not give a damn what happens to his friends who also apply. I observe these things in the premed program. Students who could mean a lot to one another cannot relate to each other because they are competing. They will even destroy one another's experiments and relay misleading information about what was said in class so that the next person fails an exam. This interpersonal violence which is rooted in structural violence is absorbed and comes out in different ways: as suicide, alcoholism, drug addiction, murder, and in violence directed elsewhere.

We need to understand violence in this structural context rather than in isolation. Once we understand violence as inevitable in an inegalitarian, competitive, dehumanizing way of life, then we will know that we cannot fight it at home. We can perhaps ameliorate it at home, and that is important. I am not saying that first aid in an emergency is not important. But when we think that all there is to dealing with violence is first aid, then our commitment to first aid may perpetuate the dynamics which make sure that we will forever be busy in first aid.

If one cares about people then one has to go beyond first aid and become involved in political movements that are willing to identify capitalism as a dehumanizing mode of production and distribution and are searching for alternatives. There is no single correct alternative. Very often people in this country think that the only way to live is either under American capitalism or under Russian state capitalism. That is an illusion. There are alternatives which people can figure out when they discover that these issues are not taboo to think and talk about and when they ask questions about more meaningful ways to organize communities and work. To me, a search for alternative modes of social organization is the only way to overcome violence in the family.

Employment and Democracy

Short range, the first policy step is eliminating the illusion that unemployment is normal or necessary for a healthy economy. Then, full self-employment which means to transfer the resources with which people work to the control of the people who do the work: self-direction, or, to use a very ancient term, democracy in the workplace. (The funny thing is that we tend to talk about our way of life as a democracy. A democracy means a way of life that is run by people. Ours is run by those who control the people's resources and not by the people.) I think we have to aim for full participation in work by all, under control by all working people in their work places. We then have to ensure that the product of work be shared in accordance with the needs of all members of communities in relation to their age, health, and so forth. Work should not be compensated at fixed rates in hierarchical terms. The reward system, whether it operates in kind or through money, ought to be geared to the needs of people and not to what positions people have succeeded to obtain, and it ought to take care of everybody. These are policies which would gradually reduce the experience of violence in everyday life and would thus reduce and eventually eliminate interpersonal violence.

* * * * *

The Uses of Corporal Punishment

—Well, specifically, I remember your [DG] contretemps with Senator Jennings Randolph from West Virginia around corporal punishment in the hearing on the National Child Abuse Center in 1973. It was obvious that what at that time was a modest proposal for social change, which we all would agree is essential for the prevention of child abuse in the family, was not something that could be talked about in rational discourse in the Congress.

DG: Unless you beat children young, they will not take the beating they have to take throughout life. I've always maintained that you rear slaves with sticks. You do not need to beat free people—their freedom is inborn. If you want a nation of obedient consumers and organization people, you have to beat them into submission.

—So you are suggesting that beating children is functional for training children for life, as well as functional for the parents in releasing their pent-up frustrations?

DG: Of course. It serves several ends. And you beat children with your hands or you beat them psychologically. Most of us beat them the psychological way, which is much more subtle and sinister. If you beat them physically they know what to hate. If you beat them psychologically through manipulation you really destroy freedom in their souls.

—Are you suggesting that children should be raised from infancy in a very laissez-faire kind of way, total freedom?

DG: This is the same sort of question that people ask when I say capitalism is bad. And they say, "So you want Russia?" The alternative to beating children is not laissez-faire, it is not neglect of requirements for healthy growing up. Hopefully, adults have some competence; children need guidance, stability, love, teaching, information, a lot of things.

—How do you differentiate guidance and teaching, which is really a form of discipline or correction, from your very broad concept of beating?

DG: Well, I think the differentiation starts with the self-concept of the adult. Is the adult an absolute authority or a participant in a community where people are at different stages of development and where there is a mutual responsibility of sharing competence and skills? I think a family is a community which can either start with respect for the developmental stage of every member, or it can start with viewing the parent as the absolute authority and sole source of knowledge and comfort and the child as an object or property.

We have to examine our feelings about our own children when they say "No." There is something that we want. When my child decides to drop out of school and doesn't want to become a professor, what does that do to me? We have enormous investment in our children as being our continuity in the life process. That causes us not to respect them, but to use them as objects. There are many ways to support and to help a child, but we tend to drift from helping them into forming them into our own image.

Equality and Authority

—I'd like to get back to your point that the violence that we see destroying families is a consequence of the larger structural violence. And I'm wondering if we can alter some of this structural violence.

DG: Well, you know the liberal solution which is implicit in what you were just saying, operates on the notion of having more equality. There is however, no such thing as more equality. You either have equality or you don't. More equality merely means having a different level of inequality. As long as you maintain inequality in the work system and in the control over resources and decision making you will have competition. And when you have competition you need to be tough to get to the top. Whenever there is a vertically organized social system you will have child abuse. The only way to eliminate child abuse is to shift to a horizontal system.

—In this family system, you seem to be arguing for collegiality as opposed to hierarchy and authority. I'm wondering how that is implemented, for example, in the socialization of children. How do you provide the authority that is appropriate for parents without exploitation?

DG: Consider Erich Fromm's notion of rational vs irrational authority. Rational authority is authority derived from competence. If you are an engineer and I am not, and I want to build a house, I will ask you to show me how to build the house. Now, if you show me how to build the house, you are making use of your rational authority over my lack of knowledge. On the other hand, if because you are an engineer with a good income you can buy congressmen who will write laws that provide privileges for engineers, then the rational authority of the engineer has become irrational authority.

Now the same is true in the family. When they were small, I knew things that my children did not know. I was an authority on soccer, and I taught them how to play it. And I had some competence in other things. But if I am acting by virtue of these limited competences as an absolute god in the family, as a patriarch, then we have shifted from rational authority to the irrational use of authority.

—Talking about equality of power and autonomy at work, couldn't we test your notion by looking at child abuse among occupations in which there is more autonomy and power?

DG: You can test these notions by taking a trip into a kibbutz and examining the incidence of child abuse. I am no advocate of the kibbutz as it now exists; however, the cooperative participatory democracy of kibbutz communities has, I think, for practical purposes eliminated child abuse and interpersonal violence. There has not been a single case of murder in kibbutz formations. I think mental illness has been reduced, but I am less clear on that. Alcoholism and drug addiction have been reduced.

—I'm thinking of looking at something that isn't a commune. It's highly unlikely that our societies are going to dissolve into small communes. What about your thinking on occupational groups where there is more autonomy?

DG: A phenomenon like child abuse is a function of total context. If you select a single element of the total context of the system of human relations, beliefs, and perceptions, and change it, then you have merely introduced confusion, and you will have perhaps worse problems. If you want to eliminate violence, then you cannot start by saying it is impossible for us to live communally. Why is it impossible? We always did until 10,000 years ago; there was nothing else. The people that lived in this country prior to the primitive Europeans had a very advanced social system, free of child abuse.

The Need for Child Abuse

—If I understand you correctly, your hypothesis is that child abuse is almost essential for our capitalistic society to continue to function.

DG: I'd say so.

—Well, it would seem then, logically, that the most abused would be the most successful, and in point of fact that seems not to be the case. It seems that those that are not the most abused tend to be the most successful in our society.

DG: Would you mind specifying what you mean by success?

—People who achieve by our social standards, the greatest amount of wealth, the greatest amount of influence.

DG: And are they happy people?

—I suspect that the president of General Motors is happier than the fellow who is in the unemployment line and doesn't have enough to eat. Happiness is a hard quality to measure. But I am really asking: if the hypothesis is accurate, why is it not true that the most abused become the most successful?

DG: That is an oversimplication of the hypothesis. I think the hypothesis would say that the most abused would become the most dependable beings that could be used by the society for further gain.

—The hypothesis is that abuse is a built-in function of our society, and as our society becomes more competitive, then abuse becomes more prevalent. I would really question that hypothesis.

DG: Let's go back to the definition of abuse and violence that I have used. It is a deficit in development inflicted by active conditions in our way of life. Now the question is whether the President of the United States or of General Motors is or is not the fully developed human being that he or she could have become. And I would say, that the people that you call successful, by and large, have developed a very narrow range of their enormous capacities to a very high degree. They are one dimensional beings. The other day I read a study asking children of top executives of the Fortune 500, whether they would like to be like their father. What do you think their response was? Most of these youngsters felt neglected by their parents (their father, primarily) and they would not want to follow that person's model. Successful people become very lonely human beings. There are no winners in a win-lose context. There is only an illusion of winning, but there are no meaningful relations, and there are no fully developed human beings. How come there are so few Beethovens, Leonardo da Vincis or Einsteins?

—Do you think Beethoven and da Vinci lived in societies where there was less competition?

DG: To me they are an index of what is possible, and would be possible on a large scale. Perhaps, in spite of the destructive dynamics, some break through it.

—At great cost.

—I'm not sure that is true at all. I think the fact of the matter is, and I don't have statistics to back it up, that a far greater percentage of children in our society have the opportunity to play instruments, to do art of all sorts, than ever had in the times of Beethoven and da Vinci.

DG: How about the native Americans? Everyone was an artist.

—I think a more substantive answer could be found in De Lone's book, *Small Futures*. This is a Carnegie Council report on issues of opportunity in the United States with regard to children's developmental outcomes. It has generated a fair amount of controversy, but basically advanced the argument, and offered fairly impressive statistical documentation to support it, that there is really very little upward mobility and opportunity in our society when you consider where children begin and where they wind up in our economic system.

—When you examine a whole society and a whole social political system, what are you comparing it to? Some fantasy ideal like Skinner's *Walden Two*? Or the kibbutz which involves a very small percentage of a very exceptional society? What are you comparing it with?

DG: I compare it to our possibilities. That is the only yardstick I accept. I compare it to our nature. We are born with possibilities that our social system destroys on a massive scale and there is no reason to do so.

—But I don't think our social system destroys it uniformly across class. I think one of the important dimensions of our society is that there are enormous differences in opportunity depending on where you were born and to whom you are born.

—On the other hand what I hear you saying is that the very system that gives the child advantages is death to his potential.

DG: I think it is important to question the assumption that the supposed advantaged segment of the population are fully developed. They are not.

—Again, compared with whom? Who do you see as so much more fully developed?

DG: I compare everyone with no one else but with their innate possibilities. I think we could do a lot better in developing our potentials. And I don't see why we should waste them.

—I think you have an interesting point that a lot of what we consider child abuse beatings basically train the children to obey, rationally to adjust to what the child's future life is going to be. And I have anecdotal evidence from working class families whose parents had told them that they had better learn to take beatings because that was what life was going to be like. But I do think that is one reason for arguing against a definition of violence and child abuse as broad as your view is. I mean, as theoretically interesting as it is to define violence as a thwarting of human potential, I think that violence serves so many functional purposes in our society that we have to distinguish between those types of violence against children that are meant to protect the children, given the society as it is.

DG: Do you want to comment on this?

—Let's take a less outrageous definition, a narrow definition of abuse and apply the same hypothesis: abuse is functional. I have listened to the debate this morning and I think that it is at the wrong level of analysis, because David's hypothesis is at the socio-structural, socio-cultural level of analysis. To test the validity of the hypothesis you have to do it at that level rather than to seek out individual deviant cases in families where children thrive. The best test of a hypothesis that a behavior is functional, is to ask to what degree the society's mechanisms to control the publicly labeled deviant behavior work. I think that the available evidence in child abuse over the last 200 to 300 years is that the systems designed to control child abuse serve better to perpetuate it than to control it. And that one wonders whether or not that is better evidence of its functional existence than whether finding employment, or occupational status, is related to thriving among individuals. I think that the hypothesis holds whether you use David's very broad, general, all-encompasing definition, or whether you just focus in on publicly labeled, publicly adjudicated cases of child abuse. The system seems to perpetuate it.

—I don't think it has escaped anyone in this room that this discussion is painful in terms of looking at our practice and raising questions as to whose needs are being serviced under the guise of servicing the child's needs. That is a difficult perspective to bring to our work that we need to think more about it in terms of the way we operate and the assumptions that we have.

DG: Social reality can be changed by changing people's perceptions. We are in the business of talking; most of our work is talking and sending messages to those with whom we work. We have to consider how our messages can reflect a different understanding of reality. While we are administering first aid, we can politicize that process by conveying to (I hate the terms clients or patients, because it immediately introduces a hierarchy) our brothers and sisters with whom we work an alternative perception of what hurts them and why, and that they aren't evil but that they are victims. But they are also victimizers, because they share the dominant consciousness of mutual domination and exploitation. The issue is to transcend that mentality.

BIBLIOGRAPHY

Fromm E: *Escape from Freedom*. New York, Holt, Rinehart and Winston, 1941.
Fromm E: *Man for Himself: An Inquiry into the Psychology of Ethics*. New York, Holt, Rinehart and Winston, 1947.
Fromm E: *The Sane Society*. New York, Holt, Rinehart and Winston, 1955.
Gil DG: *Violence Against Children*. Cambridge, Harvard University Press, 1970.
Gil DG: *Unraveling Social Policy*. Cambridge, Harvard University Press, 1981.
Gil DG: *The Challenge of Social Equality*. Cambridge, Schenkman Publishing Co, 1973, 1976, 1981.
Gil DG: *Beyond the Jungle*. Cambridge, Schenkman Publishing Co, and Boston, GK Hall, 1979.
Gil DG (ed): *Child Abuse and Violence*. New York, The AMS Press, 1979.
Gil DG: The social context of domestic violence: implications for prevention. *Vermont Law Review* 1981;6:339-362.
Marx K: Economic and philosophical manuscripts of 1844, in Tucker RC (ed): *The Marx-Engels Reader*. New York, WW Norton, 1872, 1978.
Maslow AH: *Motivation and Personality*. New York, Harper & Row, 1954, 1978.
Pelton LH (ed): *The Social Context of Child Abuse*. New York, Human Services Press, 1981.

CHAPTER 3

Sexual Abuse and Physical Abuse: Some Critical Differences

David Finkelhor

Extent of the Problem

One of the interesting features of the problem of sexual abuse is the rapidity with which it has come into public awareness. Most social problems have a larval stage that lasts anywhere from 10 to 15 years. Prior to 1977, we hardly heard anything about sexual abuse, and then suddenly there have been 12 to 15 books on the subject, television programs, and training sessions all over the country—a dramatic explosion of interest in this problem. Our notion about its scope has expanded dramatically too. For one thing, since 1977, sexual abuse has been the fastest growing of the types of child abuse that are reported in the national recording system. Studies done on nonclinical groups indicate that perhaps between one-fifth to one-third of all women are sexually victimized in childhood. And while these encounters are not all traumatic, they have a high potential of having that kind of effect. Boys, too, seem to have quite a few experiences. In my student study, for example, about 9% of the men who filled out the survey said that they had a childhood sexual experience with a much older person. Our notion about the scope of this has expanded a great deal too.

If interest in sexual abuse has exploded to such an extent, I think part of the reason is that there was already a network of people ready to adopt it, a network of people who were already interested in the problem of physical abuse. But as a result of being adopted by this network, sexual abuse has tended to be seen within the same framework as physical abuse. However, it is important to ask how sexual abuse is different from physical abuse because many mistakes can be made in thinking about identification, treatment, and prevention, using the framework of physical abuse.

Differences Between Physical and Sexual Abuse

There are six ways in which I think sexual abuse is different from physical abuse. First, physical abuse is committed in about equal proportions by men and women. By contrast, with sexual abuse between 85% and 95% of the offenders are men no matter whether we look at studies using clinical samples or nonclinical samples. This is not to say that women do not do things that can be sexually traumatic for children's development, but women do not seem to use children for their own direct sexual gratification to anywhere near the same extent that men do.

Secondly, sexual abuse occurs both inside and outside the family. Although this is to some extent true about physical abuse, overwhelmingly the main offenders in the case of physical abuse are parents. In the case of sexual abuse, although a large number of the offenders are fathers and stepfathers, a lot of sexual abuse also occurs at the hands of extended family members, neighbors, or other people like teachers and coaches who have caretaker responsibilities for the children.

A third important difference between sexual abuse and physical abuse is that in most cases of sexual abuse there is little physical trauma. Even in studies at hospital-based treatment programs where one would expect the largest amount of sexual abuse involving physical trauma, less than one-fourth or one-fifth of the cases have any physical manifestation, and usually that is something like genital irritation. In addition, actual full-fledged physical abuse is reported in only about 5% of the recorded cases of sexual abuse.

A fourth, important, and somewhat under-recognized difference, is that the offenders in the case of sexual abuse enjoy what they are doing. Many times the offender is getting physical and sexual gratification in the act of abusing.

The fifth difference is that in the case of sexual abuse the criminal justice system — police and prosecutors — are already heavily involved in the problem. They have been involved for a while and, in fact, they were involved before the social work, mental health, and medical communities. In the past they have had a somewhat misleading conception of the problem, but they were investigating child molesters and prosecuting people who committed those kinds of acts. In the case of physical abuse, although there is some involvement of the criminal justice community, unless a child is very badly hurt or killed, prosecutors and police have relatively little interest and are willing to cede this area to people in social work, mental health, and medicine.

Sixth, we are finding out that sexual abuse is, more than physical abuse, a middle class phenomenon. It does occur in lower socio-economic classes, but it does not seem to be as closely tied to social class as physical abuse. In the families of reported cases, the median income tends to be $2000 or $3000 higher than with physical abusers.

Identification of Sexual Abuse

Because relatively little physical trauma is involved, sexual abuse is more difficult to confirm than physical abuse. We cannot rely on the x-ray machine to provide evidence, and our other medical technology is irrelevant in trying to identify sexual abuse. Sexual abuse also has to do with sex, and nobody is very good at talking about it. Professionals tend not to ask questions about sexual abuse in routine encounters with children and families, and children tend to lack the vocabulary or comfort to volunteer information. Instances of sexual abuse tend to get concealed. For example, in my sample of students, two-thirds of the girls and three-fourths of the boys had not told anyone about their experiences. Identification is also complicated by the presence of the criminal justice system. There are very heavy sanctions, like jail sentences, that people have to contemplate when sexual abuse gets reported. People tend to be more reluctant to report cases of sexual abuse because these consequences are entailed.

Treatment of Sexual Abuse

There are some important differences in terms of treatment. Many treatment approaches to physical child abuse rely on the fact that most people receiving help for physical abuse are women. Our mental health and social service systems have a technology that is more effective in dealing with women than in dealing with men. Men are less amenable to getting treatment, they are less amenable to admitting they have problems, and they seem to require different kinds of psychotherapeutic strategies to be motivated to change. Moreover, because there is little visible harm, these men are often reluctant to acknowledge that they are doing anything wrong or causing any damage. In many cases of sexual abuse, offenders are getting strong reinforcement from the behavior they engage in; they are not motivated to change because that means losing something of great pleasure. In the case of physical abuse which grows out of anger and conflict situations, it is easier to motivate people to change. Substitute kinds of conflict resolution techniques can be suggested that quickly result in more gratifying interactions and short circuit the physical violence.

A third way these differences come into play is in community mobilization. In the late 50s and early 60s, child abuse was adopted by the medical profession, specifically pediatricians, as a problem of major concern. Physicians are an important pressure group. When they adopt a problem, other policy makers and professionals tend to take note. Adoption of the problem by the medical community marked the beginning of widespread concern about child abuse. Subsequent to that point, the government began to pass laws mandating the reporting of child abuse, and treatment programs got funding.

The medical community has been much less mobilized around the problem of sexual abuse. This is not just because sexual abuse is new. It is also because the medical community finds it more difficult to relate to this problem. For one, there is little physical injury and trauma involved, and physicians are generally more comfortable dealing with problems that have a clear medical component. Another factor is that being very busy, physicians do not like problems that involve many other community agencies. They risk having to testify in court or get involved in the planning of case management. Sexual abuse almost inevitably requires that kind of participation.

Another reason for ambivalence has to do with the psychiatric profession. Sexual abuse actually played an important role in the development of traditional psychiatric ideology. Freud initially identified many histories of sexual abuse in his clinical population. But then he decided that reports of sexual victimization were the children's fantasies, and he went on to develop his theory of the Oedipus complex, which posited that children were sexually desirous of their parents. So a generation of psychiatrists were trained to react to sexual victimization either by assuming it was a fantasy, or, if it had in fact occurred, by trying to work with patients primarily around accepting the fact that it had resulted from their own sexual impulses toward the parent. This was a misdirected way of working with these victims and only aggravating the trauma. The psychiatric profession has a more enlightened view of sexual abuse today.

But the fact that sexual abuse was involved, in a very particular way, in the development of psychiatric ideology makes it difficult for the psychiatric profession to mobilize readily around the problem. In addition, and perhaps more importantly, psychiatry right now is in a crisis and looking to reinforce its medical identity; it prefers to take on new problems that have a medical focus, problems that can be controlled with drugs and established kinds of psychiatric technology.

In any case, mobilization around the problem of sexual abuse has primarily come from the nonmedical professions. The innovative treatment programs have been headed by professionals from psychology, social work, and nursing. People working with sexual abuse have to recognize that they may not get the support from the medical community that they got around the problem of physical abuse.

Role of the Criminal Justice System

What are the implications for sexual abuse of the involvement of the criminal justice system? Many people in the medical, mental health, and social work fields have discomfort about the presence of the criminal justice system. They find that the criminal justice system has a modus operandi, an ideology, and a logic which is alien to them. There are many stories from clinicians about how the police or prosecutors interfered with cases, either by being insensitive to the family dynamics, being insensitive to the needs of the child, or giving too much importance to getting a conviction. We get the feeling that many mental health and social workers would like the criminal justice professionals to pack their bags and get out of this problem. But they are not about to do that, and in fact there is a strong public sentiment in favor of criminal justice involvement in this particular problem.

The programs around the country which have been the most successful in mobilizing the community and in identifying and treating sexual abuse have used the involvement of the criminal justice system creatively. They have not set themselves up as a counter-institution, but rather tried to identify the interests of the criminal justice system and find ways to include them. The criminal justice system can be involved in important and useful ways. Police can go into schools and talk to children about topics that psychologists and social workers could not discuss without alienating parents. Judges can motivate offenders to get treatment and to stop their abuse. To a greater extent than in the case of physical abuse, sexual abuse needs to be seen as a problem that calls for community organization, and linkages among institutions like mental health and criminal justice have an important function to play.

Prevention

Sexual abuse prevention is even more difficult than physical abuse prevention. The model that has been applied in physical abuse has been that of alienated and ineffective parents; social interventions that improve a family's economic conditions and build networks of social support can be fairly effective in the prevention of physical abuse.

But sexual abuse is a more complicated problem. It grows out of a set of contradictions in our culture concerning sexuality, and these contradictions are not abating. They are, in fact, growing more intense. We see evidence of it in the proliferation of child pornography, the increasing sexualization of children in the media, and the distancing of men from children that results from the rising rate of divorce.

In sexual abuse, the offenders are mostly men, both inside and outside the family. The implication is that more than being a problem of alienated and ineffective parenting, sexual abuse needs to be seen as a problem of *male sexual socialization*.

Why is it that the offenders are so overwhelmingly men? I would like to suggest three things that account for this; all of them have to do with differences between male and female socialization. First, women in our society get trained in the distinction between sexual and nonsexual affection. Partly as preparation for being the caretakers of children, women learn about nonsexual affection. With men, physical affection is withdrawn at an earlier age and only given back later on in adolescence through sex. Thus, men tend to seek fulfillment of all affectionate, nurturant or dependency needs through sexual channels. They are not comfortable with nonsexual affection.

A second difference is that men are socialized to focus sexual arousal around specific sexual acts divorced from any relationship context, whereas women tend to be more focused on the relationship in which the sexual act takes place. This makes it easier for men to sexualize relationships with children. The child has the right set of orifices to provide sexual gratification for the man. The fact that it is an inappropriate relationship may be somewhat distracting but not distracting enough to inhibit the man from seeking sexual gratification there. Women, on the other hand, find the inappropriateness of that relationship so distracting that they are unable to have sexual fantasies or arousal.

Thirdly, there is something that I call the *attraction gradient*: we train men to be attracted to persons who are smaller, younger, less powerful than themselves, and we train women to be attracted to persons who are larger, older and more powerful than themselves. On that gradient it is much less of a contortion for a man to find a child to be an appropriate sexual object than it is for a woman.

Now there are some implications here about larger social arrangements, implications for kinds of social changes that may have long term effects on the prevention of sexual abuse. First of all, some people might draw the conclusion that what we need to do is keep men away from children entirely. And although that may seem like a far-fetched conclusion to draw, I think it is implicit in some ideas that we have, for instance, that girls are preferable to boys as babysitters, and that men do not make good single parents and should not be given custody of children. Lurking behind those ideas is the imagery about men sexually abusing children. But, in fact, the implication should be the opposite: if we want men to learn the distinction between nonsexual and sexual affection, we need to get men more involved in the intimate process of bringing up children. I have a speculation, for which I have no evidence: that men who are actively involved in diapering children, for example, rarely sexually abuse them.

Secondly, I think that as we bring men up to be attracted to women who are their social equals, we are going to have a reduction in the number of men who need as their sexual partner someone who is smaller, less powerful, and younger than themselves. This will have the effect of reducing sexual abuse.

Closing on this note, I look forward to a time when men take more equal responsibility for the care of children and learn how to enjoy relationships with children without sexualizing them. I see this as an important step toward raising a generation of men who are not offenders against, but defenders of, the well-being of children.

* * * * *

—How would you define sexual abuse? Are you distinguishing sexual abuse by someone known to the child from sexual abuse by a stranger?

DF: I define sexual abuse as the use of a child by an adult or much older person for their own sexual gratification. The distinction between the children who are abused by people that they know and those they don't know is important for some purposes, for example in trying to figure out whether the child is at risk for further abuse. But for understanding why we have sexual abuse, it can be analyzed within the same framework.

—Do you treat violent or forced sexual abuse of children the same as cooperative, although coerced, sexual activity with children?

DF: Once again it depends on what purpose you are thinking about. If you are trying to figure out how much harm has been caused, or thinking about what motivation might have been involved in the offense itself, you might want to distinguish on the basis of whether there was force involved.

—I would like to register a comment that at least some people think that what you regarded as problems in male socialization are things that are biologically fixed. Men, for example, seem to have a harder time marrying off their daughters than women have marrying off their sons. There seems to be perhaps a sexual jealousy on the part of the father. It may be accounted for in terms of biological predispositions.

DF: I am predisposed against assuming that biology explains all differences in male/female behavior. Many biological explanations of differences were based on data about differences that are now changing. Many of the differences that were once thought to be so immutable are turning out to be less so. For example, the belief that homosexuality was exclusively male is turning out not to be the case. I know the sociobiologists have a different point of view, but I do not believe that much of their thinking is specific enough to account for the particular sex differences we see in the occurrence of sexual abuse.

—Some theorists suggest that sexual neglect and failure to sexually educate our children are causes of problems, and suggest that affection between family members is an appropriate behavior. Yet in some respects parents tend to go the other way, causing more psychological problems than sexual abuse. Could you comment on that?

DF: I believe that there is some truth in that point of view. Right now there are two divergent and conflicting trends in efforts to reform our attitudes toward sex. A group which primarily grows out of the old sexual reform movement is interested in making the family more sexually open. Another group, coming out of the women's movement is concerned with problems of victimization, rape, and exploitation, particularly of women, but to an increasing extent of children. One of the difficulties in this field is finding common ground. Some people who are preoccupied with the issue of sexual victimization want to reimpose repressive sexual codes that may cause a fair amount of damage. For example, in California there has been legislation to reintroduce the death penalty or life imprisonment for the crime of child molesting, much to the chagrin of the people who have been working in this field for a long time and realize that this will be no help in bringing offenders into treatment.

We need to be concerned about positive sexual socialization, in addition to being concerned about sexual victimization. These two concerns are not contradictory. For example, I found that children raised with repressive attitudes about sexuality were more at risk to victimization than other children. The dynamic fact is that children whose sexual curiosity is stifled by parents are more vulnerable to adult sexual approaches than children who have been given sexual information, knowledge and comfort about sexual matters. The latter children are also more likely to get help when they are sexually victimized.

—Will you comment on the psychological impacts of sexual victimization? Obviously an enormous group of college women, 19%, admit to one or another form of a sexually victimizing experience, yet they have reached their college years and presumably are functioning well enough. How would you interpret that in psychological terms and what would your recommendation be for clinicians?

DF: The effects of sexual victimization run the whole gamut, and unfortunately we do not have good long-term longitudinal studies. We do know from clinical work with adults who have been sexually victimized that as a result many apparently suffer long-term effects and feel conflicts about their sexuality, their intimate relationships, their family, and their own self-esteem—conflicts apparently connected with the sexual victimization. But since people who have been victimized and suffered few effects do not often come into treatment, it is hard to know how frequent the traumatic effects are.

Clinical work suggests that the effects of sexual victimization depend on a wide variety of factors including how long the victimization went on, how exploitative the relationship was, whether the relationship was with someone the child trusted such as a parent, whether it was an important person in that child's life, and how the relationship ended. For example, some children who seem to be able to terminate the relationship effectively or have taken some kind of positive action get a sense of themselves as being positive and effective individuals as a result, and that may mitigate some of the bad effects of the experience. The cultural context, what happens when the experience is discovered by others (is the child either blamed for the experience or not believed?), and later corrective sexual experiences, can also be important factors in long-term impact.

—One of the traumas that we notice in dealing with sexually abused children once the sexual abuse has come to the attention of an agency is that almost all of the affection between the child and the parents stops. Either the child is removed from the home or the presence of a public agency in the life of the family causes the father to stay away from the girl, even stop touching her, kissing her; so that a child who has had extensive affection suddenly has no affection at all from that parent. Could you comment on that?

DF: After the exposure of sexual abuse a process has to go on in which the child renegotiates relationships not just with the offender but with all the members of that family. While the decline of physical affection is a noticeable change, there are dramatic changes on other levels too. Although I am not involved in clinical work, I know that it is most important to prepare the child for the fact that that is going to happen and does not have to be permanent but that as the family members renegotiate relationships, things will change and then there will be compensatory developments.

BIBLIOGRAPHY

Finkelhor D: *Sexually Victimized Children*. New York, Free Press, 1979.
Finkelhor D: *Child Sexual Abuse: New Theory and Research*. New York, Free Press, 1984.
Herman J: *Father-Daughter Incest*. Cambridge, Harvard, 1981.
Meiselman K: *Incest*. San Francisco, Jossey-Bass 1978.
Rush F: *The Best Kept Secret*. New York, Prenctice Hall, 1980.

Russell D: Incidence and prevalence of intrafamilial and extrafamilial sexual abuse of female children. *Child Abuse Neglect* 1983;7:133-146.

Sherman LW, Burke RA: *Minneapolis Domestic Violence Experiment.* Washington, DC, Police Foundation, 1984.

CHAPTER 4

The Relationship Between Child Abuse and Parricide: An Overview

Paul Mones

Recent cases of patricide and matricide have received great nation-wide publicity and have, in many instances, been unfortunately portrayed as evidence of an alleged increase in the incidence of violent juvenile crime. Though the murders are quite disturbing, it is equally alarming that in almost every case the child was the victim of severe abuse.

This paper presents a preliminary analysis of the issues concerning the relationship between parricide and child abuse. There are two primary purposes for engaging in this discussion. The first is to encourage research in the area with the hope that such work can be used to insure that these children receive fair and compassionate treatment from the judicial system. The relationship between parricide and family violence has received scant attention from those professionals who work with abused, neglected and delinquent youths. Several recent studies have explored the relationship between abuse and violent behavior in adolescents. This paper will draw from these studies in its evaluation of the relationship between parricide and abuse. The second purpose is to encourage research, but research that is focused on a much broader subject than just parricide. By exploring the relationship between abuse and parricide, we have an excellent opportunity to make significant inroads into understanding the dynamics of family violence and into developing new methods of intervention to prevent the violence. Moreover, this research would prove invaluable in providing professionals with insight on the issues concerning the relationship between family violence and delinquency and adult criminality.

Statistical Overview of Intra-Family Homicides

Intra-family (this term will be used here to refer only to the nuclear family) homicides accounted for 13.5% (2631) of the 19,485 murders and nonnegligent homicides committed in the United States in 1982. The overwhelming number of these homicides were interspousal in nature—8.2% of the 13.5% (1599). Within this category which accounted for 61% of the intra-family homicides, 936 wives and husbands were killed. Parricides accounted for 1.3% (254) of the total number of homicides. Patricides accounted for .7% (137), and matricides accounted for .6% (117). Though this paper is focused on parricide, it is interesting to note within the abuse/parricide context that over twice as many children are killed by their parents than parents killed by their children. Filicide accounted for 2.7% (527) of the total homicides, with 1.7% (332) being sons and 1% (195) being daughters. It should be noted that the number of filicides is probably greatly underestimated because of the number of children whose deaths, though caused by child abuse, are reported as accidents. One source places this number at approximately 2000.

While the 1982 Uniform Crime Statistics Report informs us that juveniles (those persons under 18) committed 9% of all reported murders and nonnegligent homicides, the report provides no breakdown according to victim relationship by age of the offender. Therefore, there is no reported data on the age of those persons who commit parricide or, for that matter, any sub-category of murder. In order to arrive at an estimate for this number, I applied the 9% overall figure to the parricide category. I assumed that if 9% of all murders could be attributed to juveniles, then probably 9% of any one category could also be attributed to juveniles. However, I believe that this figure of 23 (9% of 254) is probably a minimum number. Since those persons under 18 probably have more contact with their parents than those persons over 18, there exists an increased likelihood that those under 18 will be involved in more familial disputes than those over 18. It is because of this greater exposure that a disproportionate number of juveniles are involved in parricide. Future research will determine the validity of this hypothesis.

Profiles of Accused Youth

This paper analyzes seven cases of parricide — six patricides and two matricides (one of the cases involves the murder of a mother and father) that have been committed in the United States in the last two years. All of the youths involved are in their teens; some have been tried, others are awaiting trial. Information on each case was obtained by a variety of research methods: speaking to the individuals associated with a case (where possible), reviewing court documents and reading news accounts. In addition, the author assisted defense counsel in three of the cases. The following synopses are not meant to provide an exhaustive discussion of all the issues raised by each case; rather each one highlights those factors relative to the issue of abuse. Subsequent research in this area would clearly require that indepth analyses of these and similar cases be conducted. Finally, for the purpose of protecting the anonymity of the children, they will be identified by letters.

A. *A* killed his father with a rifle several hours after they had an argument in which *A*'s father told him, among other things, not to be home when he returned. *A* waited for his father's return and shot him as he exited his car. *A*'s sister was in the house and was prepared to kill the father if *A* was unsuccessful. Neither *A* nor his sister had a record of delinquency or committing any other violent acts. *A* had been described by many as being an average child and a fairly good student. *A*, his sister and mother were physically and psychologically abused by *A*'s father for a number of years. The father brutally beat *A* from infancy to his adolescence. The father also sexually abused *A*'s sister and beat *A*'s mother repeatedly. *A* reported his abuse to the state, but no action was taken against the father. At *A*'s trial, the judge refused to consider testimony concerning how the abuse affected *A*'s mental state. *A* was found guilty of voluntary manslaughter and sentenced to 5 to 15 years in an adult correctional center. His sister was found guilty of aiding and abetting, and she received 3 to 7 years in an adult correctional facility. Their case is on appeal.

B. *B* killed his father with a handgun shortly after an argument. *B* had a history of committing delinquent acts, but the majority of these were minor offenses or status offenses. He had not been charged with committing any violent acts against a person. *B* had been brutally abused by his father, as had all other members of *B*'s family. These acts involved physical, sexual and psychological abuse. The state was aware of *B*'s father's abuse of him and it intervened several times on *B*'s behalf. The judge's decision was heavily influenced by the abuse factor. *B* was allowed to plead guilty to second degree murder and he received 15 years probation. The judge decided to maintain *B* on probation for that period in order that the court might monitor *B*'s treatment of his own children. The court was mindful of the fact that abused children have a better than average chance of becoming abusive parents.

C. *C* killed her father with a rifle shortly after he had come to see her (*C*'s mother and father were divorced). *C* had no record of delinquency or committing any violent acts. *C* had been sexually abused by her father for a number of years, and at her trial, testimony was offered which tended to demonstrate that she was in fact a victim of sexual abuse. Unfortunately, the court was not persuaded by the abuse evidence and the child was sentenced to serve from 5 to 20 years in an adult correctional center. Her case is presently on appeal.

D. *D* killed his father with a shotgun during an argument. *D* had never committed a violent or delinquent act prior to the homicide. *D* and the rest of his family had been severely abused both physically and psychologically by *D*'s father. *D*'s father brutally beat him and his father sexually abused his sisters. *D* originally pleaded not guilty by reason of temporary insanity. This plea was rejected by the court. The court found *D* guilty of voluntary manslaughter. While the abuse was clearly a mitigating factor in terms of sentencing, the court stated that it did not want its sentence to be construed by the public as condoning patricide. The judge clearly felt ambivalent about the case, as demonstrated by his description of D's father as the "scum of the earth" and "a man the planet Earth can rotate without nicely." The judge suspended D's sentence and placed him on five years probation.

E. E killed his mother, father and two brothers using a baseball bat and handgun. He is of average intelligence and has no reported history of committing delinquent acts. There exists evidence of abuse since early childhood, but since the case has not yet come to trial, the abuse factor can not be discussed in any detail.

F. F killed his father with a handgun shortly after his father had a raging argument with F and F's mother. F had no history of committing delinquent or violent acts. He is of average intelligence. F was brutally abused by his father since F was an infant. This abuse was of both a physical and psychological nature. Not only did F's father abuse him, but the father brutalized the whole family. The entire family lived in constant fear. F is accused of first degree murder and his case has not as yet come to trial.

G. G killed his mother and stepbrother after a long period in which he was psychologically abused by his mother. G was systematically excluded from most family activities after his mother moved in with her common law husband. G has no history of committing delinquent acts and was in fact described by many of those around him as an average teenager.

Profile Commentary

As alluded to earlier, further research in this area would require that a detailed analysis be conducted of each of these cases (and hopefully others). However, on the basis of the available information, one can discern several common themes in the above cases.

First, in all of the cases there existed varying degrees of serious physical and psychological abuse. In four of the seven cases there existed serious abuse of the youth's other family members. Interestingly, in only two of the cases was the abuse known to state authorities, and in those cases the accused youths received the lightest sentences. Secondly, in all but one of the cases the child had no history of delinquency. In the case where such a history did exist, the offenses were of a nonviolent nature. In almost all of the cases the child committed the act several minutes to several hours after the last incident of abuse. In one case the child killed his father during an argument. Finally, in all the cases the murder weapon was a handgun or rifle. This fact is not surprising considering the prevalence of such weapons in American homes. It is noted that in at least three of the cases (*A*, *B* and *F*) the victim was a gun enthusiast.

In all the cases which have come to trial the child was convicted. In none of the cases was self defense or insanity used successfully.

Observations on the Relationship Between Child Abuse and Parricide

The relationship between abuse, neglect and parricide has received very little attention in the professional literature, as has the broader related issue of the relationship between abuse and neglect and delinquency. It is noted that the interest which has been shown in these areas has come exclusively from the medical/psychological community.

Several studies have documented the fact that a significant proportion of juvenile delinquents were victims of child abuse and neglect. The National Committee for the Prevention of Child Abuse has noted that "most aggressive and destructive juvenile crimes are perpetrated by youths who have experienced abuse." One study found that 97% of the male recidivists (hard core delinquents) had a history of severe physical punishment in their home. Another study found that abused juvenile delinquents were much more likely to engage in hostile assaults than nonabused delinquents. Abused delinquents were 24 times more likely to commit arson, 58 times more likely to commit rape and two times more likely to commit assault. The study also revealed that nearly half of the families reported for child abuse and neglect had at least one child who was later taken to court as ungovernable or delinquent. In another study of homicidally aggressive young children it was found that 55% of the youth had been physically abused. Interestingly, the same study found that in 62% of the households of homicidally aggressive youths, the father had been physically violent to the mother.

A variety of interrelated theories have been offered to explain why certain severely abused children commit violent acts of delinquency. One theory postulates that an abused child learns his/her aggressive behavior from his/her parents. The children replicate their parents' primary problem-solving mechanism which is violent, aggressive behavior. The child learns that when he or she creates what is viewed as a problem, the parents respond by being verbally and physically assaultive. Unfortunately, the child's behavioral problems probably become exacerbated by the violence that he/she sees in everyday life, ie, the prevalence of cases concerning the murderous aggression of children and adolescents have also been widely explained as resulting from the child's acting as the agent of the parent. That is, the child, in committing the violent act, became the unwitting agent of the parent by carrying out what the parent could not do.

It is important to recognize that many abused children never become physically assaultive. These children also respond to their parents' aggression by becoming withdrawn and inhibitive.

Though the youths discussed in the above cases committed a homicide, it is not altogether clear that they can be classified as homicidally aggressive. There is unquestionably a category of delinquent youth with histories of abuse who can be classified as homicidally aggressive, but the youths discussed herein do not exhibit those behaviors which would necessarily categorize them as homicidally aggressive. In almost every case, the child has no history of committing a delinquent act, and none of them had any history of violent, assaultive behavior. In fact, many of these children might be more aptly described as potentially suicidal as opposed to homicidal. In one of the cases described above, after the child killed his mother and stepbrother, he gathered all the guns in the house and was going to rob a convenience store. His plan was to wait in the convenience store for the police to come and get him. Fortunately, he did not make it to the store. His plan can clearly be interpreted as a suicide attempt. After killing his mother, though he could not kill himself, he wanted the police to accomplish his execution. In another case (A), the boy stated that when he saw that he had shot his father, it felt as if he had shot himself.

An alternate but related theory which has not yet received wide attention is that the child who kills his/her abusive parent is taking that action which is most likely (in the child's perception) to prevent him/herself from being further abused. The act is one of self-preservation. In many of the cases described above, the accused child probably killed because it was evident that nobody was going to help him or her. If the child did not act, the abuse would have continued and sooner or later might have escalated to the point where the child became the murder victim.

Each of these children had no support system upon which he or she could expect to rely for assistance. All had been abused for virtually their entire lives, and not once had anyone come to their assistance. In the majority of these cases the surviving parent was either unwilling to prevent the child's abuse or was a conscious partner in the abuse. In light of this circumstance, the child could not expect his/her parent to act as a protector. Furthermore, it was obvious that the child believed that all others, ranging from extended family members to friendly adults and law enforcement or school officials, were powerless to help. Family members and others were usually fully aware of the abuse but never intervened on behalf of the child in an effective manner. In regard to school personnel and others similarly situated, a combination of the child's embarassment and his feeling of overwhelming powerlessness, makes him or her reluctant to seek help. The situation is further complicated by ignorance of the signs of abuse. In addition, there are those circumstances where, though aware, the school personnel are reluctant to intervene.

The choice of flight is not an option for most children. Many are inextractibly trapped in the home. Children, regardless of the presence of abuse, are emotionally and socially bonded to their parents. Even under the most egregious circumstances, it is impossible for many children to do what is necessary to leave home—namely to sever familial bonds. The child who leaves home must not only break the ties with his/her family but he/she must break ties he/she has with his/her friends, school, etc.

The survival rationale alone does not adequately explain why certain youths commit parricide; however, when the rage factor is considered, the act becomes more clearly understood. The aggressive behavior which characterizes the actions of many abused children is on one level an expression of the child's rage. This rage is present in both violently assaultive youths and those who commit status offenses (running away, incorrigible, etc). The abuse exacerbates and intensifies the stress associated with normal adolescent development. In abusive families, traditional support systems are destroyed and roles become (in the child's perception) inexplicibly twisted. The result for many adolescents is intense rage. Some children hold in their rage and become withdrawn; others express it by becoming either unmanageable (status offender) or physically assaultive. I believe the children discussed herein exhibit a combination of these characteristics. While some are clearly withdrawn, others act in a fashion which can be described as (for lack of a better word) average. In most of the cases the children were described as being no different than other adolescents.

Preliminary review of the cases presented here tends to demonstrate that these abused youths fall into a rather unique category of delinquency. They do not present the characteristics of either the classic status offender or the classic violently aggressive delinquent. In most of the cases described above, even considering the youths' deep seated emotional problems, they do not pose a significant threat to other members of society, nor do they present significant management problems.

The implication of the above conclusions in terms of legal theory suggests the development of a defense strategy based upon the long-term affects of child abuse on the defendant's consciousness. Depending on the facts, the attorney can marshal a defense which uses the abuse factor within the context of either self defense or a diminished capacity defense.

The legal strategy which focuses on the abuse is virtually identical to that used in cases where abused women kill their husbands or lovers. The profile of an abused woman in these cases has an amazing resemblance to that of an abused child who had committed parricide. The abused wife who kills her husband has, in most cases, never committed a crime in her life. She has been abused for a number of years, in many cases since shortly after the inception of the marriage; she has received minimal protection and support (if any) from society, and thus has few options.

It is obvious, however, that the wife is in a much better position than a child in terms of her options. The woman can call the police, seek assistance from friends or leave home more easily than the abused child. Moreover, in many areas she usually has access to a shelter. Protective shelters for abused children are practically nonexistent.

While the literature on parricide is scant, there are an abundance of articles concerning women who kill their husbands. More significantly, numerous women have successfully defended themselves by relying on an abuse-oriented defense strategy. The experiences of those who represent and counsel abused women who have killed their partners are undoubtedly very relevant to the matters discussed in this paper. It is imperative that those who work on parricide cases become intimately familiar with the literature and case law regarding battered women who defend themselves.

Conclusions and Recommendations

It is the intention of this paper to stimulate discussion and encourage research in an area which has heretofore received little attention. Though the number of parricides is relatively low, the subject provides a fertile ground in which to explore the broader issue of family violence. Members of the legal community especially are in dire need of information which can assist them to better understand and cope with the problems raised in cases of parricide (and family violence in general). Ultimately, I hope we can educate our society so it understands that these children who are presented to them as criminals, are actually victims of crime.

BIBLIOGRAPHY

Bourne R, Newberger EH: *Critical Perspectives on Child Abuse*. Lexington, Lexington Books, 1979.

Federal Bureau of Investigation: *Uniform Crime Report*. Washington, D.C., Department of Justice, 1983.

Garbarino J, Giliam G: *Understanding Abusive Families*. Lexington, Lexington Books, 1980.

Kempe CH, Helfer R: *Child Abuse and Neglect: The Family and the Community*. Cambridge, Ballinger, 1976.

Lewis D, Shanok L, et al: Homicidally aggressive young children: neuropsychiatric and experimental correlates. *Am J Psychiatry* 1983;140:2,148-153.

Martin H: *The Abused Child*. Cambridge, Ballinger, 1976.

CHAPTER 5

Family Violence:
Legal and Ethical Issues

Richard Bourne

DIFFICULT MANAGEMENT CASES

I am going to begin by presenting those cases that I think are the most difficult child abuse management cases. Then I would like to talk about what I see as the two primary legal questions: When should we intervene in families? How should we intervene in families?

One type of difficult case is the *poverty case*. For example, a child is brought in to the Children's Hospital and there has been some lead ingestion. The child was eating paint chips which can be fatal. If ingestion has gone on, there will be some physical damage. We wonder whether there has been neglect because the parents have allowed the child to continue ingesting, or at least have not tried to cut off access to the lead particles. We do not know how much of this is neglect, how much a function of poverty, and whether or not the parents are responsible at all for what has been happening with their youngster.

We had a rat bite case and we questioned whether we should file a mandatory child abuse report. Somebody said that this was the child's second rat bite. The first time the family came in we told them to put a mosquito net around the child's bed and make sure the food is in the cupboard. We told them to take precautions. The parents haven't done these things and now the child appears in the hospital with a second bite. I think the parents have been neglectful, but someone else thinks it is not fair to blame the parents because, after all, in this apartment there are lots of rats and this bite is really a function of poverty. Are the parents neglectful when the injury received is beyond their control?

These cases are very difficult for us to handle. When we intervene, we don't want to discriminate against the poor. We don't want to discriminate against any particular group. What I always ask is, how direct is the poverty to the risk? Is the cause of the harm the poverty, or some intervening factors where the parents are not doing everything possible to protect the child?

Consider, for example, a malnourished child. Is the problem that the parents cannot afford to buy food for the youngster, that they are buying food that is not nourishing, or that they spend money on other things besides food? Or maybe they just do not know how to manipulate the welfare bureaucracy; assuming that they could buy food stamps, they don't know how to negotiate the political or economic structure. Do we then conclude that if they don't know how to negotiate, they are somehow not fulfilling their parental responsibility?

A second type of difficult case is the opposite extreme and is abuse or neglect cases with *affluent families*. A physician, for example, holds his child under cold water to cool his temper and the child's body becomes frozen or very stiff. Is this a form of punishment? Or an accountant, or a lawyer, beats up his child. What does one do when that sort of family enters the hospital situation? Hopefully, the family is treated as any other type of family, considering the status, power and wealth of the parents as insignificant.

But anyone who has studied labeling theory knows that *who* the parents are does indeed make a difference in the way the cases are processed. If a poor family comes into a hospital emergency room and the child has a fracture, often the first question the parents are asked is if they have abused their child. With an affluent family the same type of injury may be defined as an accident. Who a person is is often more important to diagnosis than the nature of the injury. The greater the social distance between the professional and client, the more likely the label of child abuse will be applied.

An affluent family knows how to manipulate the system to its advantage. They hire well paid lawyers. The judges defer, and other professionals defer. It is not just that the family can manipulate the system, but once again, that professionals start behaving differently with a high status family. Sometimes manipulation isn't necessary because of the deferential behavior of the professionals involved.

A third type of problem case is the so-called *accident*. Suppose a child falls out of a window during the summer. The window has been left open and the child falls out and hits the ground below. Should a child abuse report be filed on that type of event? The parents should have had some protection on the window; but let's face it, we don't always take precautions the way we should. At the hospital we had a "shaking syndrome" case. A baby was thrown up into the air and then caught. The brain was damaged, and the child was very seriously injured. We wondered if we should file a child abuse report. Some people were arguing that this family has been traumatized and is under great pressure; that they are remorseful. Still others said, it is not proper to throw a baby up into the air. The family said they thought they could play roughly with little boy babies.

What about cases of ingestion? A child is playing outside while his father is cutting the grass with a gasoline lawn mower and the child swallows some gasoline and is brought to Children's Hospital. Children put things in their mouths. The problem is that the parents keep the gasoline in an apple juice container and of course it looks like apple juice. The physicians at Children's Hospital told the parent to keep all dangerous liquids away from his child by keeping them on high shelves. The ingestion happened again. At the second ingestion, we wonder if the parent is failing to protect the child. Another example is when a child falls out of a car seat, and the parent says, "Oh my goodness, it was an accident." Then we find out that the child has fallen out three other times. Is it an accident? Maybe the parent unconsciously desires to hurt the child.

These accident cases are very difficult for us because we want to follow the Hippocratic maxim of "do no harm." When somebody is suffering from guilt, do we reinforce the guilt by labeling acts as abuse or neglect?

A fourth type of difficult case is the so-called *life style case*. We can divide it into two categories: social situations and belief systems. An example of a social situation case is when the mother is a prostitute. Can a prostitute be a good mother? Of course she can. But what if she invites a client into her home, and the observing child receives too much sexual stimulation? The mother might also neglect her youngster if she is walking the streets.

Sometimes we tend to react to these cases not on the basis of the child being harmed, but on the basis of the way the family lives. Ethnic, racial, or socioeconomic factors influence perception. For example, a number of years ago a protective services worker who was relatively new and inexperienced complained that in a particular Latin American family the children stayed up very, very late at night—until 1:00 or 2:00 in the morning—and that one child would take care of the others. I had just come back from living in Latin America for several years, and I knew that children there often stay up very late at night, but they sleep late in the morning. And one family member taking care of other family members is not considered extraordinary. This protective services worker was probably ethnocentric in making her judgment of neglect.

Another example of a lifestyle case is the street-wise child. A 13-year-old lives in the street and can manage by ripping off things. Is this neglect by the parents? I have some good friends whose children are 14 and 15 and these parents have a very hard time imposing control. They are doing everything possible to communicate values, but the youngsters just don't listen. Do we inevitably hold parents responsible for the behavior of their children?

And then there are the belief system cases. For example, a child comes into the hospital malnourished; his parents believe in a macrobiotic diet. Is that child neglected? Or, a child is allowed to use a skateboard. More children are injured by skateboards than by inflicted injury. If a parent knows this and believes children should have access to skateboards, is he neglectful?

As another example, a child came into the hospital with pneumonia and was essentially dead on arrival. He had simple pneumonia which got continually worse and then the parents finally brought the child to medical attention. These parents didn't believe in so-called modern medicine. When the child became ill they gave him macrobiotic food, herbal tea, and some sort of enema, and then they called in an acupuncturist. Should we file a child neglect report? Some people said, "Yes, because these parents saw that their methods weren't working. And the doctors tell us that had the parents brought the child into the emergency room a few hours earlier than they did, the child would have lived. They have another child who also has pneumonia. If we don't file on the first child, who died, what is going to happen with the second child?"

Somebody else said, "But we have to respect these parents' beliefs. They don't believe in modern medicine. They did everything in their power to have their child live. They should not bear responsibility for his death."

Medical cases present a fifth type of difficult management problem. For example, parents have a child with cerebral palsy and because of their own intellectual limitations they can not give the child the maximum amount of stimulation or activity for the child to reach his potential. What do we do — take the child away? The parents are well-intentioned but they are not as able to rear children as families with greater resources. Or, take parents that are blind. We do not want to hurt or sanction them because they are blind. But, on the other hand, what if their blindness is affecting the way that they rear their children? Don't we put the children's interest before our empathy toward parental limitation?

Medical cases, however, involve more than the medical problems or the limitations of the parents. What about the limitations of the child? We have seen cases where a child has a severe congenital abnormality, is bedridden, and has been abused. Those cases devastate us. On the other hand we ask, "What would I do if I were that parent?" Imagine day after day having to see this child in bed, having to care for this child. Maybe after a while anyone would get frustrated enough to hurt, or at least to neglect, the child. We as professionals can empathize with the parent and are very much torn. And yet we cannot condone the abuse or neglect of any youngster.

Sixth, abuse cases where children have *psychiatric problems* are very hard to manage. First of all, sometimes we do not know whether there is a psychiatric problem. With physical abuse there is often some clear-cut injury. In contrast, diagnosing psychiatric illness is often intuitive and subjective. Psychological trauma is even more nebulous and difficult to identify. Is there a problem? If there is a problem, has it been caused by the parents? How responsible are the parents for what is taking place?

In my experience, psychiatrists are very reluctant to file child abuse reports. They are afraid to upset the rapport with their client and they say, "Well, as long as the client is in therapy there is no need to report anyway. We have the family engaged."

A seventh difficult case is where the parent is an *alcoholic*. Suppose we bring that parent to court and the black-robed judge looks down and says, "Now I want you to stop drinking." Is that going to do any good? Cases like this remain in the court for years. The parent goes on and off the wagon. We can't coerce or nag an alcoholic to get help, and therefore our ability to intervene successfully is limited.

There are other factors that make cases a nightmare to handle: conflicts among staff and resource shortages. The hospital may have conflicts with state protective services, or there may be conflicts within the hospital itself between the trauma (child abuse) team and another division, say the neurosurgeons, or there may be conflicts within the trauma team. Political and interpersonal differences upset sensitive case management. Sometimes, moreover, we confront a situation where if only there were day care services or the possibility of a visiting nurse monitoring the child, we wouldn't have to remove the child from his parents and place him in foster care. But because there are inadequate services and limited appropriations from the state government, we are going to have to go to court and recommended coercive dispositions. The system is often so unable to respond to these families' needs, that the work of professionals becomes ritualistic and frustrating. I think that political factors, interpersonal conflicts and resource shortages, more than anything else, cause staff burnout, and harm to families.

State Intervention: When

None of us wants social workers, psychiatrists, or lawyers hovering over families. We want to be free to raise our children the way that we want to raise our children. On the other hand, everybody recognizes the fact that the state may legitimately intervene if parental behavior falls below a certain standard.

Basically there are two positions. Some people encourage early intervention into family life. "Intervention can be very helpful. We can help support and buttress families, and therefore the fact that a protective service worker is visiting a family and providing services and support is clearly beneficial." And then other people, against coercive intrusion, say "No, we have to avoid intervening because intervention stigmatizes the family and because services to poor people are usually poor services. It is better if we just leave families alone." It is like the issue of treating juvenile delinquency. Some people say, "Intervene early. When a child is 11 years old, intervene. Because if you intervene early, you are going to prevent more problems later on." And other people say, "Don't intervene now. If you intervene now, you are going to label the child a delinquent and encourage a self-fulfilling prophecy."

Two dangers exist: underinvolvement and overinvolvement. It is obvious underinvolvement when a child is being seriously abused and is left in the home and then perhaps dies. Afterward people say, "Why didn't you take the kid out?" We had one case where a father had poured talcum powder around the baby's crib, and wouldn't allow anybody but him to go beyond the rim of talcum powder. He had a very disturbed paranoid personality. The baby was left in his care, and was killed, and afterwards the worker said, "Well, I didn't know that he was that dangerous." One extreme then, is not taking action when we should.

The other extreme is taking an action when we really do not have to — overintrusion. Historically, after any baby dies of child abuse, babies are taken from homes on a regular basis because every worker then says, "My baby may be the next child to die, and I am not going to take that risk." So we have had much premature taking of children because of worker fears of error.

State Intervention: How

There is the issue of how we intervene. I want to speak about this in terms of treatment and punishment. The meaning of the words *treatment* and *punishment* depends on who is doing the defining. I am a professional and I treat. But to clients, it may be punishment. For example, a social worker's plan may require pediatric examination, psychological assessment and home visits two times a week. The parent barely has time to breathe, but such intervention is done in the name of treatment.

Much conflict continues to exist between those who want to punish abusers and those who want to treat parents and protect children. The first group, usually from the criminal justice system, argues that abusive parents are criminals against whom the public demands retribution. Prosecution of the offender, moreover, may deter others from violence, lead to rehabilitation of the wrongdoers, and serve therapeutic goals for the child (eg, in sexual abuse cases, by convincing the victim that her father, not she, was the person responsible for the exploitation).

Treaters, on the other hand, fear that police will take over control of their cases and sabotage compassionate intervention. They resent any role strain which has them gathering information about families that might later serve as the basis of prosecution. Parents, fearing criminal sanctions, will less frequently seek help; children will suffer trauma by having to testify against their mother or father; families will suffer social stigma and economic hardship. Treaters also know that it is often difficult for district attorneys to prove child abuse beyond a reasonable doubt, the standard of proof required in criminal cases.

Gradually, however, a consensus appears to be developing that some abuse and neglect cases require police action for example, a child who died or suffered very serious harm such as the substantial impairment of a bodily organ or a child who is raped or forced into pornography or prostitution. Clearly the DAs don't have the resources to handle all cases of family violence—so the emphasis is on what cases should be selected for criminal action.

* * * * *

—You said one of your questions is when to intervene, and you said, in effect, "Don't intervene too much, and don't intervene too little." I'm curious when one would use intervention?

RB: I feel that both errors are equally bad for families. I am not sure that I can answer your question because it really depends on the facts of an individual case. I believe that despite the problems of the Department of Social Services, more often than not a sensitive protective service worker can be a support to a family. If the worker really takes into account that family or that child's needs, while the intervention may have costs, I believe that the benefits equal the costs. I believe that when a child is at risk for *severe* reinjury, or if the child has suffererd serious harm such as a fracture or burns, then the state should remove the child. If the child is not at risk for severe reinjury, I might leave him in the home. Not everyone is going to be a good parent. Some parents do slap children around, the child is not going to die from it, and probably not going to have to come to an emergency room from it. I'd leave the child there. Basically, I would intervene with the least drastic means necessary to protect the child.

—What about intervention at an earlier stage—taking notice of the family and thinking that it is potentially important to do something? At what stage would you invoke a state interest in the family?

RB: I am not worried about assessing too early. Maybe I should worry, but I see this as a "probable cause," a "show cause" hearing. Suppose a child comes into the hospital with a skull fracture and the trauma team is called for consultation. We find out that the parent's explanation is perfectly consistent—the child fell down from a changing table and it is not really child abuse, but the trauma team was called. Do we apologize for the fact that they were called? I do not think so.

That sort of intervention is necessary so that we can protect the child and we can come to a decision over time. It may turn out that the situation is perfectly benign, that the parents have not been unfit or negligent or abusive. But that first level of intervention is necessary for us to do our business. Unfortunately, because of the way that parents treat children in our society, because so many children are at risk, we may have to endure the invasiveness of initial assessment. That is my own personal bias.

BIBLIOGRAPHY

Bourne R, Newberger E: *Critical Perspectives on Child Abuse*. Lexington, Mass, DC Heath, 1979.

Bourne R, Newberger E: Family autonomy or coercive intervention? Ambiguity and conflict in the proposed standards for child abuse and neglect. *Boston University Law Review* 1977:57(4).

Newberger E, Bourne R: The medicalization and legalization of child abuse. *Am J Orthopsychiatry* 1978;48(4):593.

CHAPTER 6

Sexual Abuse: Some Practical Implications of Our Knowledge

Herschel D. Rosenzweig

TYPES OF SEXUAL ABUSE

Child sexual abuse is a phenomenon which undoubtedly has prehistoric origins. Civilization has been characterized by the emergence of social restraints against indiscriminate sexual activity in general and specifically by the prohibition of incest, however each culture has defined that activity. Although sexual involvement between children and adults has long been considered taboo — often to the extent that discussion of the subject has been prohibited — references to such activity do appear in biblical literature and records from the Middle Ages to the Victorian Era. In the late 19th and early 20th centuries, the sexuality of childhood became a subject for psychiatric scrutiny, and concern began to emerge about the involvement of children in adult sexual activity. In the past two decades, far more attention has been paid to the sexual abuse of children than ever before. Our awareness of the incidence and prevalence of such abuse, our understanding of its impact upon the developing psyche, and our ability to detect and respond therapeutically has moved forward dramatically.

It has been estimated that the actual incidence of sexual abuse of children is some 200,000 cases per year, and that up to 20% of the population is exposed to some form of inappropriate stimulation during childhood. The actual incidence in the past, of course, is impossible to assess because of under-reporting for centuries. Current reporting patterns clearly indicate that the incidence has long been far greater than realized and that sexual abuse of children appears to be increasing despite efforts to prevent, detect and prosecute offenders. This increase, which is real as opposed to being merely apparent as a result of increased reporting, seems to be related to a loosening of social mores regarding sexuality, particularly childhood and adolescent sexuality as manifested in movies, magazines and on television. There also appears to be a relationship between the increased prevalence of child sexual abuse and the dramatic increase in the divorce rate, the proliferation of alternative lifestyles, and the increase of single parent families and step-parent family structures.

The sexual abuse of children may be conceptualized as taking three forms: rape, incest, and sexual misuse. Because these forms are not always clearly defined and are certainly not exclusive, a child victim may be involved in more than one type and any particular instance may not neatly fit into any one category. Other terms such as molestation and exploitation have become familiar, but may refer to acts as varied as exhibition, fondling, sodomy, fellatio and vaginal intercourse. Nevertheless this somewhat oversimplified conceptual framework is useful in both the detection of sexual abuse and in providing services to child victims and their families.

Rape

Rape is an assault in which sexual penetration of the victim occurs against the victim's will, without the victim's consent. It is generally agreed that rape is an act of aggressive hostility disguised as sexual passion. It is often accompanied by threats of life-imperilling violence.

Children, by virtue of their status as minors, cannot provide legal consent, thus any sexual act between a child and an adult may be considered rape of a statutory nature. Being physically weaker than adults, generally sexually naive, susceptible to coercion, enticement and seduction, children may be unsuspectingly involved in sexual activity, especially if the adult is known or trusted, without the adult resorting to the violence typically employed in the rape of an adult. References in early psychiatric literature to the rape of children, often actually refer to young adults' recollections of sexual misuse and incest several years after the abusive events have occurred.

Nevertheless, the rape of children and adolescents in the violent sense does occur. It constitutes about 25% of the increase of sexual abuse of children. Approximately 45% of rape victims seen in general hospital emergency rooms are under the age of 18, and 15% are under the age of 12. The perpetrators of such rapes may be unknown or poorly known to the children or the adolescent victims. Such assaults generally occur against children who are unaccompanied but near their homes, in basements or in automobiles, by assailants who are typically within 10 years of the victim's age. Being significantly smaller and weaker than the assailant, a child may be overcome by intimidation or minimal physical force, and thus may not be physically injured. The adolescent victim, in contrast, being capable of greater resistance is more susceptible to physical injury.

The younger child is often the subject of pedophiles with pregenital sexual orientations and thus may suffer from fondling, sodomy and fellatio rather than vaginal penetration. Adolescents are more likely to be victims of a group or gang sexual assault than are younger children or even adults; thus they may suffer all forms of sexual violation as well as physical violence. Prepubertal little boys seem to be as vulnerable to sexual assault by relative strangers as little girls. At pubescence the vulnerability of the adolescent female appears to escalate dramatically.

The risk of a child contracting venereal disease from sexual assaults is great, even when vaginal penetration has not occurred. The risk of pregnancy for young adolescents as a result of rape is, of course, also considerable.

Clinical management   The rape of a child or adolescent by a complete or relative stranger evokes as intense a response in the victim's family as in the youngsters themselves. The management of such cases requires awareness and skillful handling of the resulting family crisis as well as treatment of the emotional and physical distress of the child. The child's family may be overwhelmed by anger towards the assailant, anxiety about the effects of the assault on the child, and guilt for having left the child unprotected. Paradoxically, some parents may be angry with the child for not heeding their warning or for creating trouble within the family. Distressed parents may not be able to provide the immediate support and understanding which a raped child requires. While it is appropriate to relieve inappropriate parental guilt, such guilt may not be an overreaction but may reflect the reality that the child has been insufficiently protected from predictable, avoidable danger.

The raped child or adolescent may be seen by medical personnel within hours after the event. The patient may be physically injured, often with superficial scrapes and bruises, sometimes with trauma including bleeding from the vaginal area. Although the youngster may appear highly anxious and agitated, child victims of rape may present a curiously different picture from adults. The child may seem remarkably calm and uninjured with only a tale of sexual molestation to tell, whereas the parents may be the ones who are enormously agitated and anxious. The adolescent victim of the assault is more likely to have suffered physical injury of both genital and nongenital character.

The principal indicator of rape is overt: the child relates what has happened. When no physical injury has occurred, however, the child may not relate the incident for some time. This may be due to the assailant's threats, or feelings of guilt or fear of being blamed — a common fear among children that their parents will be angry with them. The rape victim may then not come to medical personnel for days or even weeks after the event.

The acutely injured child, of course, needs immediate medical attention; however, it is still important to obtain an unhurried, calm, careful history of the incident from both the child and the parent. In the midst of crisis it is often useful to encourage the child to talk about other aspects of her life, such as school and family, prior to focusing on the trauma itself. So doing may calm an anxious child and helps to put the trauma into a context which is more familiar and safe. The examiner should gently encourage the youngster to relate completely and in detail everything that pertains to the acute situation. Questioning must be done in a nonaccusatory and reassuring manner. It is essential to anticipate the limitations of a child's language skills and sexual vocabulary. The examiner and the child may mean different things by what they say and have different words for what they mean, especially with emotionally charged sexual issues. Many children lack knowledge of scientific terms for sexual acts and organs and feel embarrassed to use slang with adults.

It is imperative to let the child know that she will be believed and will not be blamed for whatever has happened. During the initial interview, letting the child know that the examiner has spoken with other children who have had similar experiences, helps the child to feel less isolated and unusual. It is useful to explore the child's understanding of why the rape happened in order to correct unrealistic fears, as well as to gather data which may reflect on the child's real vulnerability.

Similarly, a calm and nonaccusatory approach needs to be taken with the parents who are likely to be suffering with intense feelings of worry, guilt and rage. The emotional status of the family needs to be assessed as the family's ability to provide emotional support for the child is often pivotal in determining the degree to which a rape is psychologically disabling: a nonaccusatory, sympathetic family response can do much to ameliorate an otherwise horrendous life event. At the same time the examiner must be assessing the adequacy of the family's protective capacity, recognizing that rape constitutes a breakdown in the protective environment.

When a child is raped, one must consider the possibility that the youngster has been sexually assaulted previously. Abused children may place themselves in a vulnerable position as a means of either calling attention to their plight or attempting to cope with a previously traumatic experience by risking repetition. Several cases of rape have come in for evaluation only after a second incident has occurred, sometimes in a remarkably short period of time after the first.

Celia,* a 14-year-old girl brought to the emergency ward by her older sister, related that she had gone out that evening to meet a friend, and had been assaulted by an unknown male who threatened her with a knife and indicated that he would kill her if she did not comply with his sexual advances. He took Celia to an empty apartment, raped her and forced her to perform fellatio. Celia was frightened but uninjured and when released went to her sister's home as her mother, a single parent, was not

---

* All patient's names in this paper have been changed for the purposes of privacy.

at home. Further history revealed that Celia had been raped three months earlier by three youths, one of whom had once been her boyfriend with whom she had been sexually involved. The incident of gang rape had not been reported because her mother had previously caught Celia with the boyfriend and had forbidden her to see him. At the time of the initial rape, Celia had not been believed and her story of being assaulted by three youths had been discounted. Evaluation of this case not only focused on the immediate emotional sequelae of the rape, but equally as important on Celia's vulnerability as a result of inadequate parental protection in a high risk neighborhood, the disintegration of the mother-daughter relationship, and this youngster's propensity to place herself in situations of high risk, in part, to gain maternal attention.

A complete medical examination should be undertaken in all cases of rape. Generally children are comfortable if accompanied to such an examination by a trusted parent. Adolescents who generally prefer privacy in their striving for independence, may prefer in these stressful circumstances to be accompanied by a familiar adult. They should be offered the option of being accompanied or being examined privately.

Many prepubertal and adolescent rape victims have been virginal prior to the assault. Many have never had a vaginal inspection, let alone an internal pelvic examination. Consequently, a careful explanation should be offered of exactly what will be done, questions should be encouraged, the examination should be done as swiftly and gently as possible. Swabs for venereal disease should be taken of all affected orifices. The contents of the vagina should be aspirated, without pelvic instrumentation whenever possible. If it is evident that such an examination is likely to be further traumatic to the youngster, it should never be forced. If the child is already known to a physician that person should be asked to do the examination whenever possible. Many young rape victims recall the medical examination as being more humiliating, more prolonged and more painful than the rape itself. The medical workup becomes incorporated in the child's recollection of the whole rape experience and if prolonged or painful may intensify the trauma.

Drs Burgess and Holstrom describe the rape trauma syndrome as including two phases: the acute disorganizational phase during and immediately following a rape, and the long-term reorganizational process. A similar syndrome occurs in adolescents and children as well, but is modified by the developmental state of the child and by the involvement of the child's family. The authors describe contrasts between children who react immediately in an expressive style manifested by marked signs of anxiety, agitation and somatic complaints and symptoms, and children who maintain a more controlled style in which they appear frightened, withdrawn and subdued. Both groups, however, may develop symptoms characteristic of the post-traumatic anxiety state shortly after the event.

These include muscular aches, nausea and anorexia, sleeplessness, nightmares and phobic concerns especially in reference to anything associated with the rape, including the hospital itself. The parents and siblings of sexually assaulted children and adolescents may experience a similar syndrome often manifested by guilt and intense anger which may be displaced from the assailant onto the neighborhood, the school, the police, the medical authorities, one another, even the child who was raped. Both parents and children may be preoccupied for weeks after the event, and may experience difficulty functioning in school work and usual family activities.

The physician's or rape counselor's anticipation of these reactions, preparation of the family by telling them how they may be affected during the next few weeks, and follow-up inquiries about whether, in fact, these sequelae have occurred, may be enormously helpful in alleviating stress. After a terrifying and highly abnormal experience it is often helpful to be reassured that at least one's reaction is normal and with appropriate family support and counseling, will pass. It is also important for the counselor to be alert for fantasies which both parents and children have following a rape, such as the fear that the child is ruined for life, will become promiscuous, will become homosexual or psychotic. Corrective information and reassurance should be offered as needed. It is equally important to listen to real fears, including possibilities of pregnancy and venereal disease, to offer reassurance and, of course, prophylactic prevention wherever this is indicated.

Incest

A child or adolescent may be even more likely to become sexually involved with a member of his or her own family as with a stranger. Incest in the most limited sense refers to sexual involvement between blood relatives. Incest in the psychological sense refers to sexual activity between unmarried members of a family rather than merely the biological parents and siblings. Consequently, step-parents, uncles, cousins, even parents' friends may be included under the rubric of potentially incestuous partners. Investigators generally agree that the vast majority, approximately 75%, of the sexual abuse of children occurs between children and either a family member or someone else well known to the youngster. Such sexual activity may not be violent and may not involve actual sexual penetration, but may be more insidious, chronic, subtle and destructive.

The revelation of incest invariably complicates dealing with the acute situation with issues of divided family loyalty, anxiety about prosecuting a family member and disruption of long- term family relationships. Incestuous relationships usually develop slowly; incest invariably indicates preexisting family problems including multiple stresses, marital disharmony or disruption, role reversals between parents and siblings, and the evolution of inappropriate sexual activity between family members. Even when intercourse does occur, sometimes repeatedly over several years, it may not be the actual sexual activity which precipitates the crisis but rather the undeniable revelation of this activity.

Incestuously abused children may attempt to alert others long before their situation is recognized. Many, however, carry the secret into adulthood. Dr Finkelhor's study indicates that close to 20% of female college students recall some form of inappropriate sexual experience in their youth, often involving family members. A remarkable aspect of Finkelhor's findings is that for the most part these experiences were never revealed to outsiders. A child or an adolescent may, in fact, disclose incest after the activity has gone on for a long time. Many children have great difficulty telling parents of such events, fearing disbelief or blame or anticipating that the revelation will destroy the parents' marriage or the family's stability. Children often feel that they have tried to tell someone by dropping some vague hint or by hoping that by virtue of her presumed magical mind-reading powers, a loving mother should already know. Sexually abused children may, on the other hand, be very explicit in describing their experiences, but may be disbelieved. They may even be punished for telling such tales.

Experienced investigators have concluded that a child or adolescent relating such information should always be taken seriously. Children rarely, if ever, make up allegations of incest. Even when distortions of perception, ulterior motives, or sexual misunderstandings are taken into consideration, one should assume that any child who makes such a report has almost certainly been sexually overstimulated if not actually molested.

Disclosure may be deliberate, such as telling a school nurse or counselor when the youngster finds the sexual activity no longer tolerable or when the perpetrator has become overly possessive or intrusive in the youngster's life. The revelation may be accidental, such as an inadvertant slip to a friend, or a confession to a boyfriend. A youngster may retract a complaint after realizing the consequences of the revelation, but such retractions are more likely to be contrived than the original allegations. The energy invested in keeping incestuous activity a secret is stark testimony to the shame, guilt and anxiety which incest engenders even in unwitting and unwilling children. Consequently, detection is often a result of a high index of suspicion on the part of professionals who encounter such youngsters.

Incestuously abused children may present a wide variety of covert signs that suggest sexual misuse and abuse within the family. Some indicators are unequivocal, such as pregnancy in socially isolated or apparently sexually inactive youngsters.

Debra, a 16-year-old girl, was referred to the sexual abuse team shortly after giving birth to a full-term infant. This shy, withdrawn and apparently intellectually limited adolescent seemed to the staff social worker an unlikely prospect to be sexually active, let alone precocious or promiscuous. In view of the fact that this youngster's denial had been so profound that she had been oblivious to her pregnancy, it was not surprising that she was initially unable to identify the baby's father. When a more comprehensive social assessment revealed that she had few extrafamilial social contacts, no boyfriends and little apparent sexual interest, the social worker became increasingly curious about the possibility of intrafamilial sexual activity and confronted both the young mother and her parents with her suspicions in a direct and nonaccusatory manner. Although Debra herself persisted in her contention of ignorance regarding the infant's paternity, her own father acknowledged with remarkable candor that he indeed was the child's father. Now free of the responsibility of the revelation, Debra confirmed her father's claim in a story of familial role reversal and prolonged incestuous activity. Although the family appeared conventional and intact, Debra's mother apparently had gradually withdrawn from her previous maternal role under the aegis of increased work responsibility, and the superficially affectionate relationship between Debra and her father became increasingly eroticized and intimate. In this case the revelation and the incestuous pregnancy produced a significant emotional upheaval in the family, and obliged family members to reassess their relationships with one another. Debra's mother expressed eagerness to accept the major part of the maternal care of the infant as a grandchild and thus through this baby, once again assumed the primary maternal role in the family. Debra had great difficulty dealing explicitly with her feelings about the incestuous relationship itself, but was able to initiate psychotherapeutic work dealing with her social isolation from peers and anxiety about new responsibilities as a mother. Debra's father, although repentent and vowing to abstain from further sexual involvement with his daughter, also had difficulty exploring the dynamics of that relationship and the feelings which had led to the incestuous activity, as well as his feelings about his daughter's pregnancy with his child. Ongoing individual therapy for Debra, and individual and family therapy for the parents has been undertaken.

The detection of venereal disease in a prepubescent child must also be considered a sign of sexual contact, more than likely made within the home. Foreign bodies in the vagina, rectal, or ureoral orifices of young children should be viewed with high suspicion of sexual overstimulation. Vaginal or penile trauma in young children should also raise questions of sexual misuse. Trauma to sexual organs may be inflicted by children who have been overstimulated or initiated by their elders.

More subtle behavioral signs, however, may be the only indicators of familial sexual abuse. Depression for no apparent reason, poor school performance, and withdrawal from friends often characterize the behavior of shy, sexually abused girls locked into symbiotic pathological family relationships.

Assertive youngsters who have been abused may become deliberately provocative, their speech, clothing and behavior becoming highly eroticized. Even preadolescents may manifest highly sexualized speech, excessive and indiscriminate masturbation, and sexually provocative mannerisms, as a means of communicating their prococious enlightenment and as a manifestation of their sexual preoccupation. Such behavior makes such youngsters particularly vulnerable to further sexual activity and abuse both within and outside their families. There is a tendency to perceive victims as no longer innocent and thus "fair game" to others.

Boys abused in sex rings, particularly, may attempt to master their sense of degradation by identifying with the aggressive initiator of the activity and sexually abusing other children. The first sign of sexual abuse in such boys may be provocative, precocious and sometimes predatory sexual activity. In effect, one form of sexual abuse may be the first sign that some other form has previously occurred.

Robert, a 15-year-old youth was referred for a psychiatric evaluation after having allegedly molested two preschool girls on a Sunday afternoon in a large recreational area near his mother's home. The boy, when confronted by the victims, tearfully acknowledged his assault, but attributed his behavior to a combination of being intoxicated and high on drugs. Further history revealed that the boy's parents had been divorced for several years, and that on the afternoon of the assault the boy had been visiting his mother who had a history of alcoholism. Robert regularly lived with his father who had married a former prostitute and whose homelife was characterized by a great deal of open sexual behavior, including availability of pornographic literature and erotic apparati, to which the boy had been exposed for several years. He had also been directly victimized five years earlier by another adolescent who had forced him to perform fellatio under the threat of revealing his involvement in some minor delinquent activity. Although placement in a residential treatment facility and intense psychotherapy was recommended, Robert instead, sadly enough, was placed in a foster home. During the first six months of his probationary stay, Robert raped several young women. He was then remanded to an inpatient psychiatric facility for long-term intensive treatment.

One form of incestuous activity which has long been ignored is that which occurs between siblings. Sibling incest is often passed over as innocent sexual curiosity and exploration and considered benign by many authorities. Studies of normal populations even suggest that sibling sexual exploration may be considered beneficial. Careful examination of reported cases, however, often reveals the existence of a great deal of individual psychopathology in both siblings and parents as well as home environments characterized by emotional neglect and sexual overstimulation, if not episodes of sexual abuse of the children by others.

A 4-year-old, Molly, the youngest of seven children in a single parent home, was referred after a culture of her vaginal discharge proved to be gonococcal. There was no adult male in the family and her mother denied any recent contact with any of the children's fathers, or any current boyfriend. A survey of the family revealed that Molly's 16-year-old brother, a handsome, swaggering young man known by the family to be very active sexually, was perceived by Molly's older sisters as an enormous pest and tease and was constantly bothering them in a flirtatious, if not explicitly sexual, fashion. Throughout the family interviews, the older girls spoke jocularly and scornfully of their older brother's alleged exploits, while Molly, who was restless and active, engaged her brother in a physically playful manner with considerable enticement to rough-house and tickle. The children's mother, a warm and concerned woman, appeared to be exhausted by her children's demands and activity level and clearly unable to control the superficially playful, but intense, sibling interactions. The older boy's physical prowess, size and outgoing personality clearly cast him into a position of being the household's dominant figure whose presence affected everyone. He was also the dominant male, seen to be in competition with his mother for control of the family mood and level of agitation. Although direct sexual contact between Molly and her older brother was vehemently denied by the boy and his mother, gonococcal screening revealed that he too had a positive culture. Rather than dwelling on the futile pursuit of a confession for that which seemed fairly obvious if not acknowledged, therapy focused on the family dynamics which might foster incestuous activity between the siblings.

Many children often involved in incestuous activity reach a point of intolerance and simply leave home. Adolescent runaways may present a litany of complaints about their parents, but often omit the most glaring stress from which they must escape: the sexual activity which has been imposed upon them. Shelters and agencies serving runaway children report histories of incest in some 15% of their clients. Some sexually abused children develop other signs of serious psychopathology, and require both medical and psychiatric hospitalization as a means of avoiding the intolerable situation at home. Symptoms may include hysterical seizures, anorexia nervosa and bulimia, and impulsive, aggressive and defiant, or depressed and suicidal behavior. A recent study by Graham Emslie and Alvin Rosenfeld revealed a 37% incidence of interfamilial sexual abuse in children and adolescents who had been hospitalized for psychiatric conditions that initially appeared to be unrelated to sexual abuse. When the issue of whether these youngsters had been sexually misused within the family was pursued, the alarming incidence was uncovered.

Clinical Management A youngster is often helped to reveal the long hidden secrets by the gentle probing of a patient, nonaccusatory and supportive adult who is able to hear whatever unpleasant truths may emerge, without condemnation, revulsion, or overreaction. Because talking about personal sexual experiences may be extremely difficult for many children and adolescents, it is sometimes useful to encourage them to write to the interviewer describing what has transpired. In one case, a youngster had a secret about which she simply could not speak. A great deal of effort to help her talk about it proved fruitless, so she was encouraged to write her therapist a note. The next week a 20-page document was received in which the patient spent 19 pages digressing about all sorts of other things and, finally, it was as if she said, "I'm so exhausted I can't write anymore and the only way that I can stop is by putting it in black and white," she revealed the incestuous activity that had been on her mind for such a long period of time. Many children will come in and say, "I can't talk. I can't tell you what is happening." And when encouraged to write, they will say, "OK, but don't look." And then you turn your back and they will write the tell-tale note. This is a useful way of helping children to free themselves from their enormous anxiety and inhibition.

The attitude of the interviewer is always extremely important, for child victims of incest are often exquisitely sensitive to any indication of shock, embarrassment, or blame by the adult who they must trust before they can reveal the existence of such disturbance in their family. It is striking how often the readiness of the interviewer to hear the possibility of sexual abuse is directly related to the readiness of children to confide the real problem. As we talk with mental health clinics, we are struck by people who tell us, "I just don't see this. I just haven't heard of it. Are you sure that it is as prevalent as you say it is?" When they begin to become attuned, to feel free to talk about it and free to allow themselves to hear it, they begin to hear it and become more able to encourage youngsters to communicate.

SEXUAL MISUSE

The third category that I referred to is a much more general category than incest itself. That is the category of misuse. Everything that we have talked about is considered misuse in a broad sense of the word. It has been defined by Drs Brant and Tisza as referring to any sexual activity which is inappropriate for a child because of that youngster's immature age and development and because of the child's role in the family. Although much broader in scope than incest and perhaps less clearly defined, sexual misuse is an enormously helpful concept, bringing into consideration cases of sexual molestation and overstimulation which would be excluded from even the broadest definition of incest. Misused children may be fondled or masturbated or enticed to sexually stimulate adults without necessarily being engaged in coital activity. They may be indiscriminately exposed to adult sexual activity, sometimes by multiple individuals, sometimes involving psychosexual pathology. These children may be engaged in provocative sexual games, child pornography or group activities, or encouraged in sexual exploration with other children for the benefit of a pedophiliacally inclined adult. They may simply be neglected and thus allowed to observe or participate in whatever sexual activity occurs in their environment. Sexually misused children often manifest all the signs and symptoms ascribed to the victims of actual incest, and although their experience may appear less acutely traumatic, the long-term effects in personality formation and interpersonal relationships may be as disruptive as the effects of incest.

CHARACTERISTICS OF ABUSING FAMILIES

Although there is no such thing as a typically abusive family, there are a number of characteristics commonly found in families in which sexual misuse and incest occur. Many of the parents have been victims of sexual misuse in their own childhood. Many of their marriages are fraught with serious conflicts, sexual problems in particular. Often one parent or both have an alcohol or drug abuse problem. The parent of the same sex as the misused child is often absent from the home for long periods of time, especially at night. Such absences may be ascribed to work, illness, or simply the pursuit of the parent's own interests. Although no family configuration is immune to sexual abuse, so-called blending or reconstituted families, especially those with periodically changing step-parents and single parent families appear to constitute particularly vulnerable environments. Some surrogate parents may not experience the same degree of emotional prohibition in expressing sexual impulses towards children who are not biologically related as they might feel in a relationship with their own offspring. Children with unwed parents may be exposed to a greater degree of eroticized courtship behavior in parents and parent's friends than children in conventional, two-parent households. Psychologically, the parents of sexually misused children are often relatively immature and dependent and may encourage role reversals, in many ways asking that their children assume more parental responsibility than is developmentally appropriate. A sexually misused child often appears to be inordinately attached to the family and unable to separate adequately to develop social relationships and an independent identity. Separation can only occur by breaking or running away. Although these characteristics may be found in many dysfunctional families in which sexual misuse does not occur, when a child from such a milieu also manifests some of the covert signs of possible sexual abuse, our suspicion and concern should be alerted, and further more explicit inquiry encouraged, albeit with discretion.

MANAGEMENT SUGGESTIONS

Once sexual abuse has been suspected, management becomes a major problem. The physician must obtain the most comprehensive possible and must not hesitate to include inquiries regarding sleeping arrangements, open versus closed door bathroom practices, relative modesty versus nudity in the family, and the degree of privacy and discrimination regarding sexual activity. Candor by an inquiring physician often evokes remarkable data regarding familial sexual interactions. If overtly inappropriate sexual activity is clearly suspected as would be the case in venereal disease in a prepubertal child, a direct appeal to the parents to consider all possible contacts is indicated. The physician should seriously consider the parents themselves. Direct confrontation with adult members of the household with the physician's suspicions must be done delicately after carefully considering the potential of those confronted for acting out. Impulsive behavior and poor judgment is often characteristic of sexually abusive families. The physician must consider the potential of family members for acting punitively towards the child who has revealed, even inadvertently, a well kept family secret, or for acting precipitously in a self-destructive manner. Some families have bolted not only from treatment but from the state when advised of a physician's concern. In one case an accused grandfather suffered a mysterious but fatal boating accident a few weeks following the revelation of incestuous activity with his granddaughter. The dangers of either overzealous intervention or avoidance of dealing with the issues are very great indeed.

In all states there are now laws which oblige professionals to report any case of suspected child abuse including sexual abuse. Physicians and other professionals are obliged to report suspicions to child protective agencies and the police and may be subject to significant penalty for a failure to do so. The police and the child protective service units have the authority to investigate such reports. Reporting is done by phoning, followed by submitting a written report detailing the reasons for suspicion. Physicians often feel that filing such a report will violate his obligation of confidentiality. Suspected child abuse, however, is one situation in which that obligation is waived. Mandated reporters often fear that overzealous Children's Protective Services (CPS) case workers may disrupt family integrity and remove children without due cause or process. Reporters should be made aware that permanent removal of children occurs in relatively few reported cases, fewer than 20%, and that far more effort is made to provide protective and supportive services to families in an effort to foster family cohesion.

Engaging abusive families in a therapeutic program designed to protect their children is often very difficult. It is only when such families have been engaged in vigorous treatment over a period of time, however, that one can begin to alleviate the damaging psychological effects of abuse and assure that relapses into a destructive pattern of interaction will not occur.

Sexual abuse affects all members of a family. The familiar concept of a perpetrator-victim dyad is simplistic and misleading. When an abuser is a parent or parent surrogate, the spouse plays an important role in family dynamics, sometimes perpetuating the incestuous activity. Marital problems and particularly sexual problems must be addressed in therapeutic effort. Parental absences, either physically through separations, employment, illness, or emotionally through depressions, psychosis and preoccupations contribute to the sexual abuse of children. Alcoholism may be a contributing factor in either parent. Sexual abuse of a child may serve some secondary gain for other members of the family and thus may be ignored, tolerated or even encouraged to keep the family intact. Familial sexual abuse is often associated with significant role reversals, such that the abused child is given adult and even parental responsibility of a wholly inappropriate nature. Siblings may also be affected, sometimes being abused themselves. They are often keepers of the family secret. They may be victims of parental neglect or of the role distortions contributing to or resulting from incestuous relationships. Those who manage or attempt to treat these families must be aware of the complexity of the family interaction and must be prepared to deal with the effects upon the entire family.

A wide variety of treatment techniques have been employed with sexually abused children and their families. Perhaps the variety speaks to the lack of any one sure response. Individual psychotherapy for both parents, whether the parent is a perpetrator, spouse, or mere bystander is essential. Adolescent victims and younger children may benefit greatly from crisis intervention and in long-term therapy. Dyadic therapy has been helpful in many cases, especially for mothers and daughters, and family therapy involving a particular youngster and both parents as well as all members of the immediate family has also been useful. Therapeutic groups for adolescent victims of rape and incest, groups for mothers of abused children and for male perpetrators of sexual abuse have been highly beneficial to many individuals. The Parents United and Daughters and Sons United models by Giaretto have demonstrated the effectiveness of these approaches.

These families, however, often revert to their familiar defenses of denial and avoidance. Therefore, the continued involvement of an external authority (such as the district attorney's office or the Children's Protective Services), even though such an authority may be intrusive and potentially persecutory, is often essential to assure that treatment will take place.

Fundamental in the treatment of incestuous families is the helping of the adults to accept full responsibility for their inappropriate involvement and to avoid projection onto the child. Perpetrators must establish genuine remorse, often stated as an apology to the child, and must make as a major commitment in their lives the avoidance of such interaction in the future. Whatever the treatment modality, the therapist must have well defined therapeutic goals. Abusive families may present a morass of psychopathology which can engulf the therapist. The most immediate treatment goal must be to assure that further abuse of the victim and other children will no longer occur and to prevent retaliation for disclosure. This may necessitate temporary removal of the youngster from his or her home or temporary removal of the offending adult. Ultimately, however, another treatment goal should be to sustain the family as a unified group whenever possible. In order to maintain family unity one must attempt to correct deviations in the adult psychosexual orientation, the children's emotional development which may be affected by the abuse, and the intrafamilial condition which predisposed the youngster to becoming a victim. The therapist must strengthen nonabusive bonds between parents and children and parental protectiveness. One must also address ancillary factors which contribute to the abusive situation, such as parental depression, social isolation, marital conflict, absenteeism, alcoholism, dependency and any other psychological or social factors which contribute to the role reversal, neglect or misuse of the children.

In order to treat sexual abuse effectively, professionals must overcome their own sense of horror, outrage, disgust and anger, and be aware that such painful feelings may evoke in them strong defenses of denial, rationalization and avoidance when confronted with the signs of sexual abuse. It is often difficult to believe that the pleasant, apparently caring family sitting in the outer office is actively engaged in the intense drama of incest behind the doors of their home. Only when one can dare to consider the possibilities which have been unthinkable can sexually abused children and their parents be spared the anguish of persistant, displaced, destructive sexual activity.

BIBLIOGRAPHY

Brant R, Tisza V: The sexually misused child. *Am J Orthopsychiatry* 1977;97:80-90.
Burgess AW, Groth AN, Hostrom LL, Sgroi SM: *Sexual Assault of Children and Adolescents*. Lexington, Lexington Books, 1978.
Emslie GJ, Rosenfeld A: Incest reported by children and adolescents hospitalized for severe psychiatric problems. *Am J Psychiatry* 1983;140:708-711.
Finkelhor D: *Sexually Victimized Children*. New York, Free Press, 1979.
Finkelhor D: *Child Sexual Abuse: New Theory and Research*. New York, Free Press, 1984.
Herman J: *Father-Daughter Incest*. Cambridge, Harvard, 1981.
Meiselman K: *Incest*. San Francisco, Jossey-Bass, 1978.

CHAPTER 7

Assessment of Incest

Gretchen Graef
Beverly Weaver

The Sexual Abuse Treatment Team deals with all kinds of sexual abuse: intrafamilial sexual abuse, commonly known as incest; sexual assault of children by people not known to them; and sexual assault of children by people known to them but not family members. We also see some assailants. We will not be able to cover all of these situations here so we have selected the topic we think is most talked about both in the literature and in these seminars, and that is intrafamilial sexual abuse or incest.

Recognition

In order to recognize child sexual abuse one must be willing to entertain the possibility that it exists. That is the most difficult task in this work. Incest is blanketed in secrecy, denial and repression. Practitioners, victims, and abusers are all affected by these symptoms. Part of the task is to raise awareness about the symptoms. But that is only step one; then it is necessary to use the known information.

We will start with the more obvious. The child may share the secret with a friend or trusted adult in spite of the pressure and the prediction of dire consequences. These children are often warned by the parent that they will be removed from the home or that something dreadful will happen which will distress and disrupt the family. The child may, in a moment of angry betrayal, when her father refuses to grant a special privilege, tell her mother. Or the mother may note other signs of diminished respect for the father by the child. The mother may arrive home unexpectedly and witness some part of the abuse or notice tell-tale signs. Family members may begin to notice obvious and complex strategems designed to help the daughter avoid being alone with the father.

If this is a young child, there may be obvious imitative sexual play with peers and/or siblings which is sophisticated beyond any reasonable childlike sexual exploration. This play may take extreme forms of chronic, overt masturbatory activities as anxieties mount beyond manageable thresholds. One 3-year-old seen early in our work here at Children's

Hospital was placing objects in the vagina and the rectum of the family cat. There may be sexualized speech and play in the course of otherwise regular play (for example, playing house, playing with a doll or drawing) and of a too explicit nature to be initially denied.

The reason we say *initially* is that we get many disclosures which are made when one parent, with a certainty that something is wrong, brings the child in and presents what he/she has noticed. Three to five weeks later this parent begins undoing all that he or she has known by saying, "Well, the drawing didn't mean that. That was an overreaction. That could be anything. That could be a rocket ship." (However it happened to have a glans on the end of it.) It is disturbing to watch people as the denial and the repression of information begins to set in. These symptoms are not always indicators of sexual abuse, but they often are. Unless one carries within him/herself the awareness that it can be intrafamilial sexual abuse, he/she is more inclined to miss that than not. Venereal disease in a child should always be regarded as the consequence of some kind of sexual abuse or misuse. Complicity in the myth of toilet seats and bed sheets is a regrettable stance for the medical profession.

Sexual Abuse Assessment

The possibilities of intrafamilial sexual abuse, with overt or covert indicators, should be pursued in an orderly and sensitive manner. A directed social and developmental history should be obtained as it would be in any good medical or socially oriented practice and service. The history would include areas such as special relationships, onset of symptoms and/or regression, and details about sleeping and child care arrangements. Assessments should be made of the adequacy of adult protectiveness across the board, not just in the area of sexual misuse, and of the possibility of danger to siblings, an area which is often forgotten.

The child should always be interviewed, and our point of view is that the child should be interviewed separately from the family. Children will not talk about sexual involvement with a family member unless a safe and neutral environment is provided. Nurses and physicians can be quite expert in helping children adjust to strange and anxiety ridden settings, such as emergency rooms, as quickly as possible while playing with stethoscopes, tongue blades, puppets and dolls. When an alliance is formed, one can guide the play, drawing, and/or conversation towards the area where information is being sought. We have worked with protective service workers who, after an initial engagement of the child would say, "sometimes adults do things to children, like touch them on the private parts of their body, down there," and point to them to make sure that the child understands. "Will you tell me if someone has been touching you? Or if you have been involved in that kind of play?" The results can be amazingly direct. During moments of stress children can be surprisingly candid, particularly if they are engaged and have the capacity to trust and relate, which many children do.

If a thorough medical exam has not been provided or has not preceded such an interview, even if the results are less conclusive than desired, this examination must be done.

While there is a national trend to eliminate legal requirements for corraborative evidence of sexual assault against children, it is unfortunate that with the absence of any corroborative evidence a child's statements cannot carry sufficient weight in a court of law. The younger the child, the greater the need to try to corroborate his or her story.

On the Sexual Abuse Team, we often help prepare children for this physical examination. Contrary to belief, these children generally tolerate such procedures well and are often relieved to hear the doctor or nurses assure them that "everything down there is OK." In general, visual examination of the genitalia for females and a knee-chest position for males and the same position for a rectal examination with bright lights is the one that is utilized. Most of the equipment used is a swab and a culture. These children are not subjected to speculum exams unless it is essential and unless there is an indication of trauma and/or bleeding.

* * * * *

—Could you comment on how you begin when an alleged abuser comes into your office?

GG: By feeling nervous. I say that "our understanding is that this has taken place." And then I sit back. I don't get into, "you did," "I didn't." I finally say "Well, I think that something happened. We don't hear this or see this when it hasn't occurred. Would you agree that you are at least in the running?"

I've actually had fathers say to me, "Well, yes, I see your point, I guess you have to consider all the possibilities." And that's all I need— one logical entry point, and then we can begin to talk about what goes on in the family.

Unfortunately, in this kind of situation we have to deal with the reality that the process of providing help is a potentially dangerous one, and that in the process of providing help and hopefully moving the family to a healthier position, there may be pain and distress. In medical practice one sometimes does painful things to help somebody get better. A surgeon may do a painful procedure or may insist upon painful exercises or unpleasant medications. But he or she is firmly convinced that it will lead to a better condition in the long run.

There are several different schools in this business. There are people who are enormously confrontive. They put the couple right into the room and ask what is wrong with the marriage that would allow this to happen to this child. The underlying belief is that focusing the issue where it truly belongs—between two adult people who have distorted or abnegated their parenting role—serves the child. And then there is the other point of view which is more of a child guidance model, a more careful, gentle, and speculative and perhaps a less productive one immediately.

BIBLIOGRAPHY

Finkelhor D: *Sexually Victimized Children*. New York, Free Press, 1979.
Finkelhor D: *Child Sexual Abuse: New Theory and Research*. New York, Free Press, 1984.
Herman J: *Father-Daughter Incest*. Cambridge, Harvard, 1981.
Meiselman K: *Incest*. San Francisco, Jossey-Bass, 1978.

CHAPTER 8

Children's Somatic Expressions of Family Dysfunction and Family Violence

Linda Gudas

Children's manifestations of anxiety and concern regarding family dysfunction may often be observed in a variety of common somatic complaints. The population of children who present with symptoms such as enuresis,* encopresis,† stomach aches, headaches, school problems and feeding and sleeping disorders are possible examples of such manifestations. These symptoms are frequent occurrences among children and, although difficult to assess, deserve careful consideration and comprehensive management from all child care professionals.

Although these complaints are commonly seen in many of the clinics at Children's Hospital, the course of the symptomatology is usually not representative of the general pediatric population. As a referral center, the hospital tends to see those children who are treatment-resistant; that is, such children have often been to several providers and experienced a variety of unsuccessful treatments. Parents and professionals alike are frustrated and confused. When, as frequently happens, the child is referred to a medical clinic within a hospital, it is important to consider that the parent or provider has elected a medical rather than a psychiatric, neurological or surgical setting, alerting the professional to the perspective in which the referral source has chosen or prefers to view the complaint.

Abdominal pain is a common complaint which occurs in approximately 10% to 20% of school-aged children (Apley, 1975; Galler, Neustein and Walker, 1980) and may be organic as well as psychobiological in nature. The following two cases illustrate examples of each type of etiology.

---

* Bedwetting, may also refer to daytime wetting (diurnal enuresis).
† Fecal soiling, usually secondary to chronic constipation that is not of physiologic origins.

Two Case Illustrations

Jeff, aged 9, was brought into an emergency room complaining of stomach aches of two days' duration. His mother was upset and could not do anything to lessen the pain. Blood chemistries and urinalysis were unremarkable. Abdominal examination revealed no major abnormalities. Jeff's mother volunteered information regarding four similar attacks of pain and related these episodes to stressful home situations, ie, birth of a sibling, separation between parents, a geographic move and the start of school. Family history additionally revealed that Jeff's father was recently hospitalized for treatment of severe alcoholism. The health professional told the mother that Jeff's examination was negative, that she should not worry, and that the boy was probably reacting to his father's illness. Forty-eight hours later, Jeff returned to the emergency room still complaining of feeling very ill. The diagnosis at that time was a ruptured appendix and the child was taken to surgery. As Jeff was wheeled to the operating room one of the surgeons turned to the mother and said, "Why didn't you bring him in earlier?"

Tom, aged 12, was taken to his primary care clinic because of intermittent abdominal pain of six months' duration. His parents described his attacks of pain as excruciating. Physical examination, radiological findings and laboratory tests were within normal limits. Except for his stomach aches, Tom appeared to be a healthy, happy, active boy. While taking a history from the child, the health professional discovered that Tom's grandmother had died of cancer eight months previously. She had lived in Tom's home and the child had been very upset when she died. Upon asking Tom what he thought might be wrong with him, he stated that he didn't know, but the pains were like the kind his grandmother had. Careful follow-up was arranged for Tom. During his frequent visits to the center, he was examined, reassured that he did not have cancer like his grandmother and helped to understand the reasons for the stomach aches that were now subsiding.

When a child complains of any kind of repeated somatic symptoms, parents are encouraged to seek medical care. If an organic cause or significant psychopathology is identified, the child is treated with defined methods and protocols. If, however, no physiologic or blatant psychogenic cause is evident, the child may be labeled as experiencing nonorganic pain or functional pain and is often dismissed from the medical system.

The fact that medical providers often fail to consider relevant social, family, developmental and behavioral data that are important diagnostic information is exemplified in a retrospective study undertaken by Brant and Tisza (1977). Searching for chief complaints or diagnoses that might lead one to suspect sexual abuse, these researchers reviewed the records of patients presenting to a pediatric emergency room with the complaints of molestation; rape; incest; sexual abuse; painful urination; genital irritation, trauma or infection; and adolescent pregnancy. Note that these symptoms are very clear cut—not vague general stomach aches, or headaches. Out of 56,000 emergency room visits, 52 possible sexual abuse cases were identified. Fewer than five of those had been reported to the hospital sexual abuse team. According to the medical records, professionals had not considered sexual abuse in at least 25% of these thousands of visits. Although recent legislative and professional as well as lay awareness of this problem has encouraged health care providers to address these complaints more comprehensively, an appalling lack of consideration of critical personal and social factors continues to exist.

What happens, then, to the child who is told that nothing is wrong, and there is no need for further treatment? The child still experiences symptoms, and a functional diagnosis helps neither the child nor the family. On the other hand, an organic or a psychogenic diagnosis really does not view the child from a biopsychosocial framework but rather looks at the child in an either-or fashion, isolated from multifactorial and transactional issues and influences.

A Developmental Perspective

How do children develop symptoms, and what makes these symptoms occur at different developmental stages? In answering these questions, one must address the child's chronological age, level of psychosocial and psychosexual development, the cognitive functioning of the child, and the child's role in his or her social and family milieu.

In terms of somatic symptoms, infants usually present with feeding and sleeping disorders and may be failure-to-thrive babies (Berwick, 1980). Responding on a sensorimotor level of development, these babies may demonstrate persistent lethargy or hypermotility and irritability. They frequently do not engage in social play. Toddlers and preschoolers also present with sleep disorders, often in the form of night terrors or frequent waking. Autonomy issues, particularly around separation and toilet training, are characteristic. Problems with speech development, notably expressive language delays, are common. This child thinks in terms of phenomenalistic causality (Elkind, 1976); magical thinking is rampant and there is belief that events that happen together cause one another.

In school-aged children, thinking is concrete although cause and effect relationships begin to be understood. Children's worries and concerns are often presented through specific symptoms, and their responses are visceral in nature, such as stomach aches, constipation, bed-wetting, and vomiting. It is not until early adolescence that the child can think abstractly and understand that his/her body is telling him/her something. Eating disorders, social problems and clinical depression may be observed in these children.

Child Development, Sexual Abuse, and Child Symptoms

A 5-year-old girl who had been forced into oral sex by her assailant first came to the medical system presenting with a problem of vomiting. What was revealed after numerous sessions was that the assailant had ejaculated in her mouth and the penis had lost its erection. Her cognitive understanding of what had happened was that she had swallowed the penis. Thus, she responded by repeatedly vomiting. An 8-year-old girl who also had been assaulted one night masturbated to the point of wetting her pants. She was confused, upset and cognitively did not understand what had happened. Her concrete conception of her sexual assault was that the semen was urine. Here she had wet the bed after self-stimulation. Was she growing a penis? What was happening to her?

Adolescents present with complaints associated with more mature levels of cognitive development. Headaches, for example, are common, and they are not the "my head hurts all over" kind that a school-aged child may describe. The adolescents' specific descriptions of their symptoms may be diagnostically confusing. Sexual acting out may occur, leading to pregnancy. Anorexia nervosa may develop. Noncompliance may start to manifest itself in adolescents with chronic diseases such as asthma and diabetes.

Family Troubles and Child Symptoms

Jane, aged 7½, came to the school function program for academic delay in reading and math. She did, in fact, have learning difficulties. But her medical history revealed that she had been encopretic since age 4; she also complained of frequent stomach aches occurring mostly in the evening. Her parents spoke freely of their open relationship with their children. It was not unusual for the children to see their parents bathe, toilet, or be intimate. Jane and her 12-year-old brother continued to take baths together and sleep in the same bed.

Janes's symptoms illustrate the two conditions inherent in the perception of pain. The first is a biological function serving to alert the individual that something is wrong independent of emotional, cultural and environmental factors. The second condition is the communicative meaning of pain — what the patient is trying to say beyond the fact that she/he is in pain. What was Jane trying to communicate through her ongoing encopresis and nightly abdominal pain?

In viewing psychosomatic symptoms as a family affair, Minuchin et al (1975) postulate two hypotheses: 1) certain types of family organization are closely related to the development and maintenance of psychosomatic symptoms in children and 2) these symptoms play a major role in maintaining family homeostasis. "Since family interactions affect the psychophysiology of the child in a psychosomatic crisis, disorder is seen as situated in the feedback process of child and family."

According to this model, family processes that encourage somatization are basically threefold. In one, the child is, in fact, physiologically vulnerable. In the second, the human relationships in a child's family takes one of the following forms: enmeshment, overprotectiveness, rigidity, or lack of conflict resolution. In the third, the sick child plays an important role in the family's pattern of conflict avoidance, and this role is an important source of reinforcement for his/her symptoms.

The case of a child who is truly physiologically vulnerable can be viewed in two ways. On the primary level would be children who have a preexisting physical disorder, such as asthma or diabetes, that had been occurring before or during the actual stress. Secondly, vulnerability can be viewed as cases where there are no predisposing factors in evidence and the psychosomatic illness becomes apparent in the transformation of these emotional conflicts into somatic symptomatology.

The four family transactional characteristics are defined (Minuchin et al, 1975) as follows:

Enmeshment is a high degree of responsiveness and involvement between family members. Changes in one family member or in the relationship between two family members effect the family system. Boundaries are so weak that a member has no clear life space. The notion of boundaries is important to keep in mind when observing family interactions — those implicit and explicit rules that govern relationships between family members. When roles and boundaries between parent and child remain clear, the chances of enmeshment are diminished.

Overprotectiveness occurs when family members' perceptions of each other are structured around protective issues. Self-preservation and preservation among family members is common. For the symptomatic child, the experience of being able to protect the family by using the illness may be a major reinforcement. Expression of the symptoms yields secondary rewards.

Rigidity is maintaining the status quo or resistance to developmental changes within the family structure. The family is unable to grow or change. Avoidance circuits must be developed, and a child who is a symptom barrier is a useful detour. Such families are described as living in a chronic state of submerged stress often presenting as healthy, untroubled families. The only problem is the child's illness. This type of family will say, "Everything would be OK if only Johnny would stop wetting the bed."

Lack of conflict resolution, the final transactional pattern, is based on how the family deals with enmeshment, overprotection and rigidity issues. These families avoid conflict at all costs.

A child in the sick role can be caught in a variety of patterns. Minuchin et al (1975) comment on three. In *triangulation* the child is put in a position where he/she can not express himself/herself without siding with one parent against the other. The child will do anything necessary, including being ill, to maintain the stability of the family. In *parent-child coalition* the child tends to move into a stable coalition with one parent against another. This pattern may be seen, for example, in families of divorce. In *detouring*, the spouse dyad is united and the parents submerge their own problems in a posture of protecting or blaming their child. Again, the symptom which the child presents is defined as the only family problem.

The following case presentation beautifully illustrates the model Minuchin et al (1975) describe:

> Kate S. was involved in an incestuous relationship until she was sixteen. When she was nine, her father crept into her bedroom one night and "began fondling my genitals. I woke up because it was uncomfortable. I told him it hurt, so he stopped and explained my body to me. That was the first time anyone told me I had a vagina. My father was the household god — the absolute authority. All decisions went through him, and it didn't occur to me to question him.
>
> "Until I was twelve or thirteen and entering puberty, the incest was infrequent, but always when my mother was at home. My father, under the guise of teaching me what sex was and what other men would do to try and move in on me, would call me to his . . . He had my cooperation. I was very passive. On some level, I knew it wasn't right because he didn't want my mother to know. He said it would distress her . . .
>
> "But I had an investment in our relations, too. My father shared confidences with me, he'd talk at length with me. He wanted to be close with me as he wasn't with my mother. They couldn't communicate he said, but he didn't want to leave her. And I wanted very much to be close, to touch, to have an intimacy I missed with my mother. My mother was too embarrassed to even hug my sisters and me." [Kinkead, 1977, p 172].

Kate, now in her 30s, spent her adolescent years severely depressed and remains emotionally scarred.

The Choice and Maintenance of Symptom

What are the dynamics regarding choice of symptomatology? Why does one child develop encopresis, another bed-wetting? Green and Solnit (1964) believe that the psychological tasks that the child and mother are focused on at a specific developmental level determine the symptomatology. The attainment of toilet training during the stage of autonomy is a classic example. Thus, the choice of symptomatology is related to both developmental issues and family organization. An interesting finding in some families is that members other than the symptomatic child may also experience somatic complaints or excessive concerns with bodily function.

Examples are numerous such as the nutritionist who has an obese or anorexic child or the parent with an irritable bowel who has a child with constipation.

What about precipitating events and the development of symptoms? A somatic episode may well manifest itself differently during various periods of a child's and family's life. In addition to experiencing symptoms at any specific time, it is important to determine what crises the parents or other siblings may be going through. Stress within the family may cause its members to protect its own homeostasis. At the point where the family feels disequilibrium, the child becomes symptomatic and the family unites in concern and protection, and the system gets rewarded on some level. Then the whole cycle begins again.

What about the system maintenance? The family may become entwined in a repetitive cycle of protection, concern and secondary gains. Green and Solnit (1964) state that the child senses the parent's expectation of his/her vulnerability. The threat is converted symbolically and displaced to a body system or function with the child perceiving the problem on a physical level. Thus, a definite symptom arises to focus attention and avoid the danger of the true problem. It is safer to have a stomach ache than to have the family address the father's alcoholism, the marital discord or the sexual abuse.

Diagnosis: Three Cases

What about identification and assessment of somatic symptoms which are the result of family dysfunction? Occasionally, the family problems are presented during the initial interview, as is shown in the following two cases.

Joey was a 5½-year-old boy referred to Children's Hospital by his kindergarten teacher for evaluation of lack of academic progress and recent noncommunicative and withdrawn behavior. His mother described him as recently whiny, clinging and demanding to sleep in her bed. He was experiencing nightmares. Both the school and Joey's mother related the onset of the problem to violent and abusive interaction between Joey's parents. Three months earlier the child observed an incident where his father severely beat his mother and threatened to blow her head off with a gun. At the time, Joey's father was in a local correctional institution undergoing evaluation.

The second case involves two siblings. A girl aged 9 and a boy aged 10 were brought to the medical clinic for evaluation of similar, multiple complaints: abdominal pain, bedwetting, encopresis and lethargy. The onset of these symptoms were gradual and correlated with a six-month period of physical and sexual abuse by two babysitters. The family was involved in court action, and the children were scheduled to testify.

In these two cases, the children were brought by parents who clearly stated the major crisis in the family. What about the child with the somatic complaints where the family dynamics are unclear, or unknown, but there is just an uneasy feeling that all is not well?

A case in point is a 10½-year-old girl who was referred to the medical clinic after a six-month period of enuresis and encopresis. The child's medical record documented one previous contact with the hospital four years previously when the child had come to the emergency room with a chief complaint of vaginal itching for one month. The child's mother casually mentioned during the interview that this girl's 19-year-old sister was being seen at the same time in the gynecology clinic for a postabortion follow up visit. When a medical work-up on this particular child revealed no obvious cause for the child's symptom, the gynecology nurse who was seeing the 19-year old sister was contacted to elicit further family data. It was revealed that the 19-year-old had been raped four years previously which was two months previous to this child's visit for vaginal itching. The 19-year-old sister had since had three abortions. According to the gynecology nurse practitioner, the effect on the family had been pronounced. That information was obtained solely through the mother's comment about the daughter's appointment in another clinic.

These cases lead me to focus on interviewing and history-taking. The beginning step in recognizing cases of family dysfunction is an openness to consider the possibility that such a situation exists. There are times when a physician is busy, tired, hassled, and has other patients waiting. In essence, he/she just doesn't want to hear about and deal with family problems. At times like these, the physician should either arrange for the child and family to see a professional who can address such issues or schedule a follow-up visit at a time when he/she can be more receptive. He shouldn't ignore his feelings that something is going on in this family.

The interview with a symptomatic child involves the parents as well as the child. Parents often feel that the child's behaviors are a reflection of their caretaking. In exploring the history of the presenting problem then, both the parents' and the child's perception of the symptom should be elicited. Parents and child may be seen together, separately, or a combination of both methods, depending on the needs of the individual members. Asking children why they think they have come to see you yields a plethora of responses and cues you into the way the child views the problem. One child, for example, who had a long history of encopresis responded to the question why he came by stating, "because I fell on my knee yesterday and I hurt it." His mother revealed later, in private, that the child never would have come if he had known the truth. Clearly, this type of response sets the interview off on a much different level than one in which the child embarrassingly admits, "I messed my pants," or refused to talk. A general sense of how the problem is being perceived within the family is provided by the asking of this question.

Ask children to elaborate about their symptom and to use descriptive language in explaining how, and where and when it hurts; what it feels like; and what they think is wrong. Rather than putting words into the child's mind by asking questions such as, "Is the pain sharp or dull?" attempt to elicit an explanation in the child's own terms. As with the case of Tom, whose grandmother had died, the child's description of the pain helps to elucidate both the importance of the symptom to the child and a beginning awareness of the problem.

Exploring parents' perceptions of the how, where and when of the symptom is also crucial, and comparing the similarities and differences in the child's and parents' responses may provide valuable diagnostic information. Questions which may be important to focus on are: Does the symptom occur at any specific time or place (ie, never in school, only at night, on weekends when visiting the father)? What other symptomatology is occurring that may be related (ie, learning problems, school avoidance, other somatic disturbances)? Has this symptom or have similar symptoms occurred with the child or any other family member before?

A picture of the chronological development of the symptom is helpful, such as when it first occurred and its increase in frequency. In searching for the initial onset of the complaint, careful history-taking does not merely begin with the symptom onset but at the start of the child's life. An early, significant event can remain active in the lives of family members and become part of future development experiences. Important historical information may be elicited by asking about the mother's pregnancy and the child's early infancy. Questions could include: How was this pregnancy for you? Were you ready for the baby? Were there complications during the pregnancy, labor or delivery? Attempts at determining what any complications meant to the parent may give clues as to how the parents perceived risk factors in the child. It is also important to remember that a minor complication to a health care provider is not necessarily minor to a parent. Did the parent believe this child was healthy at birth? Parental reactions to early events may influence the child's future developmental progress.

In exploring growth and developmental milestones, parents may offer important perceptions of their child. Comments such as, "He never wanted to be with anyone but me" or "I knew I'd have trouble from the moment she began toilet training" are diagnostic of what kinds of issues have been focused upon.

When interviewing the child, there are two techniques that the provider may use which are easily administered and frequently provide a wealth of data. One is the Draw-a-Person test (Goodenough, 1926; Koppitz, 1968; Machover, 1949). The person or boy or girl that children create is often revealing (ie, who and what they draw) as well as helpful in providing a sense of the child's developmental level. The other technique is to ask the child to draw a picture of the family doing something. This drawing is particularly useful if you sense family discord.

An example of the use of such drawings is the case of a 7-year-old boy, who was brought to the medical clinics by his aunt, uncle and father for a problem of night-time enuresis. When the child was undressed, notable bruises and scars were noticed down the child's back, buttocks and legs. The father reported that the child was punished by the mother in one of three ways for wetting: he was beaten, forced to go outside until his pants dried, or he was locked in the basement. The child was asked to draw me a picture of his family doing something. After initial resistance, he drew a straight, horizontal line across the middle of the paper. In the lower right-hand corner he illustrated a staircase, spiraling downward. There were no people. When asked to describe the picture, he pointed to the left side and said, "My mother is in the kitchen. She's cooking." And then he pointed to the bottom, near the staircase and commented, "I'm in the basement and the door is closed." When asked what he was doing there, he put down his pencil and left the table. One painful disciplinary method had been clearly drawn.

Puppet play or dollhouse play may also provide insight into family dynamics. The provider may participate in such play or merely observe what the child does. Puppets may be of clear gender and age (such as a boy, a girl, a man and a woman or may be caricatures or animals). Dollhouse play may be used if the child's symptom is focused around a particular daily activity such as toileting, eating or sleeping. By going through a typical day in the household, one can observe how the child uses (or does not use) the bathroom, what happens at mealtime, bedtime routines and who sleeps where.

Many health care providers are skeptical about using such techniques, believing they should not be analyzing a child's drawings or play methods. However, these techniques are not used in this context in a strict diagnostic sense but are helpful in information-gathering and assisting the child to communicate through play. Interpretations should be guarded. Later on, it may be interesting to talk about how people feel about nontherapists doing this.

During the physical examination, the reaction of the child to the overall procedure as well as to each organ system is significant. What kinds of questions do they ask? Where does the child focus his/her attention and does this relate to the presenting symptom? Is the child responding in a developmentally appropriate manner? Is a child more anxious or submissive than you would expect? An illustrative example is the case of a 4-year-old girl who presented to the clinic with a six month history of intermittent abdominal pain. She was generally cooperative until her heart was examined, when she became anxious. The abdominal exam was even more anxiety-provoking, and then she repeatedly pushed the provider's hands away. During inspection of the genitals, however, she responded by complete submission. Her response alerted the provider that something was wrong. After several visits with this girl and her mother, it was discovered that some sexual exploration among neighborhood kids had been occurring over the previous months. These episodes had been disturbing to the child and she reacted by having tummy aches. The diagnostic clues which this girl offered in her reactions during the physical examination came from looking at this child within a developmental and behavioral framework.

Parts of the physical examination may be deferred until a later time if the examination of those parts is anxiety-provoking and if the family is compliant in returning. A classic example is the rectal exam. While this may be a necessary procedure with a child who presents with abdominal pain or constipation, you may not have to do it on the initial visit, but rather suggest that the child return in a few days. A 3-year history of abdominal pain or encopresis does not have to be fully evaluated and cured in one visit.

The quality of the parent/child interaction throughout the visit should also be assessed. Does the parent dress the child? What kind of safety or protective measures are used? Does the parent place the child on the examining table and then walk away or hover near the child during the entire procedure? How do the parents prepare the child for painful procedures? How do the parents and child interact during these uncomfortable procedures?

Management

Finally, the management of children with somatic symptoms must be addressed. Medical intervention is, of course, required in nearly every situation and is an imperative, first-line consideration. The enuretic child, for example, must be screened for infection and anatomical defects. Children who are referred for psychotherapy deserve initial medical evaluation, even if the symptom appears to be emotional in nature. Collaborative efforts of the medical provider and the therapist are critical to a comprehensive plan of care.

Therapy of a psychodynamic nature with children experiencing somatic symptoms needs to be directed at changing the family process that maintains the symptoms as well as changing the use of the symptom by the child and family. This task is not an easy one. We need to consider whether the problem is one that can be managed with a single provider and, if so, from what discipline or whether multi-disciplinary or consultative help is necessary. There are some children who I will not actively treat until there is some kind of psychotherapeutic intervention. In such cases, I am concerned about what the symptom means and how it has maintained the homeostasis of the family. The answers to these questions are usually best addressed through interdisciplinary team efforts.

* * * * *

—I have a question in terms of management. Do you ever use behavioral modification methods?

LG: How are you defining behavior modification?

—In terms of giving rewards.

LG: In some situations, yes, and in other situations, no. I think that behavioral techniques need to be individualized. Consultation with a behaviorist should always be considered an option, especially for assistance in consistent use of the technique. I do believe that behavioral modification should not be the only method used for these children as the approach addresses only the symptom, not the underlying reason for the problem. I do apply some of the principles of behavior modification in management. Specifically the use of rewards is often helpful. Consider the child who has been encopretic as a result of withholding stools. Once such a child's constipation is resolved and a regular pattern of defecation is established, the child may use a calendar or diary where she or he can check progress, such as sitting on the toilet or doing some self-care such as putting his or her underwear in a basket in the bathroom. The child may log the progress in a diary and be rewarded for being responsible. A case where I had more difficulty with using rewards is with a child who is nocturnally enuretic. This child has no conscious awareness or control over the wetting, and I think that a strict reward system for dry nights is unfair. Positive reinforcement such as verbal praise like, "You had a dry night; that's super" is fine but the child should not feel denied of a reward for wetting.

—I want to ask how to generalize your approach to other nurses and physicians. Particularly with regard to physicians, I'm concerned that they have neither the time in an individual office to do this kind of work, nor often the personal maturity and support system that enables them to reckon with child and family data much less forming relationships with children and parents that enable them to do this kind of work. What are your reflections about the process of training physicians and nurses and also about their interactions with social workers whom one would think would more naturally be the ones to address the family material if not the direct interview and treatment of the children?

LG: Let me answer first by saying that I think this kind of approach is the basis of nursing. In most nursing curriculums, family dynamics, interactional and social science concepts are strong. I think that medical education will never really address this except very briefly and such training usually comes on a post-graduate level. At the least, awareness that some of these symptomatologies suggest underlying problems should be formally addressed in a medical school curriculum. If physicians are trained to recognize that a problem may exist, they can find the appropriate people, such as social workers, to do the interviewing or the management if they feel unprepared or unwilling to do so themselves. Clearly, it would be unfair and unjust to expect a house officer in the emergency room to interview, assess and manage a rape case from beginning to end. It is the people who ignore or do not identify these problems that concern me.

—As difficult as assessment is, I think treatment is more difficult. I am wondering how you keep these families involved, particularly when there is such an investment in the illness, the secondary gain aspect of the homeostasis. And when it is a psychiatric problem as opposed to a medical problem, you have to have them change their definition of the situation. How do you do it?

LG: Cautiously. That relates to what I said initially about these families or their health care provider choosing a medical setting to present the problem, frequently because a psychiatric diagnosis is too threatening. I follow one little girl in the second grade who is enuretic, encopretic and electively mute—she does not speak outside of her house. The parents very clearly told me there is nothing wrong with this child except her enuresis and encopresis and warned me not to address emotional issues. You deal with whatever the family will let you deal with at the time, and gradually move towards where you feel the problem is. If you do that carefully and cautiously, the families remain engaged. The reason that particular family with the electively mute child was at Children's was the family had repeatedly been told that the child needed some medical management for the enuresis and encopresis, but the child had severe emotional problems and that was the source of her symptoms. The parents heard that on the first visit and never came back. I saw this family eight or nine months ago and they are still engaged—not as well as I would like, but there is still contact with the medical center. I have even been allowed to contact the child's school. I believe they still come only because I did not hit what was the most threatening, vulnerable point in that family's history.

— I'm wondering about the cognitive as well as emotional factors.

You mentioned the child whose grandmother died of cancer. And I am wondering how frequently you find that it is a misperception that can be clarified with a small amount of information?

LG: You have to look at the cognitive functioning of the child, but you also have to look at what the child has been allowed to perceive by the parents. The child may, in fact, be cognitively aware. Deaths may occur when the child isn't home, or the death may not be explained. And the child wonders what happened to Grandma. Grandma used to be here and isn't here. "Is Grandma sleeping?" "Well, you know, Grandma isn't here anymore." What does that mean? And the child keeps saying, "When will I see Grandma?" "Well, Grandma isn't here anymore." "Well, where is she?" "She's not here anymore." That child is asking cognitively for more information but the parents can't give it. It causes stress everytime the child asks where Grandma is. The disequilibrium in the family comes out. The parents get stressed. Their own grief comes out. The child's symptom arises. That is not simply a cognitive misperception, it is a combination of the two.

—I'd like to respond to the cognitive question. Although you are adding on another dimension of it, which is what the children have been told and what they are allowed to perceive, I think it is also important to remember that children do not think like adults. And particularly younger children think very differently. So very often it is not simply a question of the child's misperceiving and of telling the child or giving the child the wrong information. Because younger children think differently, it is important to understand the nature of that thinking. The most important thing to remember is that the children under the age of 5 or 6 are egocentric. What that means is that they understand events in the world only through their own lens. And that thinking is quite rigid. They really cannot step outside and see how an event could happen independently of them, and independently of how it affects them. So, for example, a child who has lost a grandmother really may not be able to comprehend that that loss occurred independently of the child. Independently, perhaps, of the time that he or she misbehaved when the Grandmother asked her to be quiet and the child wasn't quiet. So they feel, egocentrically, that their behavior must have caused it. Also, a child at preschool age cannot understand what death is and cannot understand the irreversibility of the absence of an individual. Giving correct information is not going to make children think differently if they are developmentally unable to utilize the information. But sometimes helping parents to understand the child's cognitive level and why the child can't understand what death represents or why the child can't separate or understand that he or she wasn't connected to that death, might help them to cope with the child and give the child time to make his or her own developmental growth towards a more adequate under-standing.

BIBLIOGRAPHY

Apley J: *The Child with Abdominal Pain*, ed 2. Oxford, Blackwell Scientific Publications, 1975.

Berwick D: Nonorganic failure-to-thrive. *Pediatr Rev* 1980;1:265-270

Brant R, Tisza V: The sexually misused child. *Am J Orthopsychiatry* 1977;47:80-90.

Elkind D: Cognitive development and psychopathology: observations on egocentrism and ego defense, in Schopler E, Reichler R (eds): *Psychopathology of Child Development: Research and Treatment*. New York, Plenum, 1976.

Galler JR, Neustein S, Walker WA: Clinical apects of recurrent abdominal pain in children. *Adv Pediatr* 1980;27:31-53.

Green M, Solnit A: Reactions to the threatened loss of a child: vulnerable child syndrome. *Pediatrics* 1964;34:58-66.

Goodenough FL: *Measurement of Intelligence by Drawings*. New York, World Books, 1926.

Kinkead G: The family secret. *Boston Magazine* October 1977:100.

Koppitz EM: *Psychological Evaluation of Children's Human Figure Drawings*. New York, Grune and Stratton, 1968.

Machover K: *Personality Projection in the Drawing of the Human Figure*. Springfield, Ill, Charles C Thomas, 1949.

Mastrovito RC: Psychogenic pain. *Am J Nurs* 1974;74:514-519.

Minuchin S, Baker L, Rosman B, et al: A conceptual model of pyschosomatic illness in children. *Arch Gen Psychiatry* 1975;32:1031-1038.

CHAPTER 9

Obesity, Family Violence and Medicine

William H. Dietz
Denise Bienfang

We would like to preface two cases with a brief review of the epidemiology and health effects of obesity. Obesity is a highly prevalent disease in this culture. Current estimates place 5% to 25% of all children as obese. Age of onset seems evenly distributed throughout childhood. Remission rates decrease with age; for a child aged 5 there is a high likelihood that the child's obesity will remit by age 15; if a child is obese at age 10 the likelihood that the child's obesity will remit is much lower. If a child is obese at adolescence there is an estimated 80% chance obesity will continue into adulthood. Rates of spontaneous remission are related to severity. One Swedish study estimates that once a child is 160% to 170% of ideal body weight, the likelihood of remission is almost 0%.

Most people are familiar with the psychological effects of obesity; people who are obese in childhood and into adolescence tend to have a lifelong negative self-image. Obesity in childhood has significant associated health effects as well. The orthopedic effects include slipped capital femoral epiphysis (a hip problem). Whether this results in increased osteoarthritis in adulthood is not known. A second disorder which is associated with obesity in children is Blount's disease, a growth disorder of the legs associated with severe bowing which may produce a lifelong deformity and require surgery. Among the respiratory effects of obesity is the Pickwickian syndrome named after Fat Joe in the *Pickwick Papers*, who was constantly falling asleep. It used to be thought that this disorder was primarily hypoventilation which caused carbon dioxide retention. A more important cause is sleep apnea which is due to the fat in the back of the throat occluding the airway. The mortality of this disorder is about 25%. Nonetheless, only 14 cases have been reported in the literature to date. While the prevalence of hypertension is quite low in childhood, 50% of all children with sustained hypertension are obese. Outside the Pickwickian syndrome, sudden death as a consequence of obesity is unusual in children.

Twenty-five percent of type II diabetes mellitus in adults is attributable to obesity, 75% will develop maturity onset diabetes mellitis. In a seven year follow-up of adults who were in excess of 200% of their ideal body weight, 25% of those individuals died within seven years of diagnosis. Together, these data emphasize that obesity in children, particularly advanced obesity, is not a benign disorder.

At the heart of the mechanism for obesity is an energy intake in excess of the expenditure. That is the bottom line regardless of metabolic background. Although a lot of attention has been paid to metabolic defects there is little evidence that these are causal. They may enhance susceptibility or promote persistence of the disease, but they are not causal.

The major correlates of obesity in children are within the family. There is an increased risk of obesity in children with obese parents, older parents, divorced or separated parents, or in families in which one parent has died. There is a strong association with birth order — the younger the child is, the more likely that child will become obese. The larger the family the lower the likelihood of obesity within the family; only children have a higher prevalence than children in families with more than one child.

Obesity and Family Function

In the three years we have worked in the weight control program, we have become increasingly aware that obesity may be an index of family dysfunction. The two cases we will present illustrate this problem.

The first case we will call Richard, a boy now 5½-years-old referred to the weight control program 18 months ago for severe obesity and bowed legs. At that time his weight was 214% of ideal. Hospitalization at age 2½ failed to disclose a physiologic basis for his obesity, and outpatient dietary therapy had been unsuccessful.

Richard was the second child of a diabetic mother who suffered a psychosis requiring a four-week hospitalization shortly after his birth. He had been living with his grandparents and four of the mother's siblings, three of whom were massively obese. His grandmother was 53-years-old and suffering from obesity, hypertension, diabetes, and the Pickwickian syndrome. His step-grandfather was a 54-year-old alcoholic who also had diabetes and heart disease. According to Richard's mother, both she and Richard's grandmother were abused by her stepfather. She reported that she slept with a knife in order to protect herself from him until she moved into her own apartment. Additional history revealed that Richard was the family's pet. He was called "big man" by his grandparents who gave him money and free access to the local market. At one time he threatened his mother with a knife because she refused to give him money to buy food.

Physical examination revealed a moderately hypertensive, massively obese boy in excess of 200% of ideal body weight, who fell asleep several times during the interview. This is characteristic of children with the Pickwickian syndrome; initially the only clue may be this daytime somnolence.

He was enuretic* and encopretic.† His legs were severely bowed due to Blount's disease which produced a waddling gait.

We elected to hospitalize him as soon as possible. The morning after his hospitalization, his grandmother died and we discharged him to permit his adjustment to her loss. Six weeks later he was admitted to the Psychosomatic Unit. Their assessment was that the mother and maternal step-grandfather were unable to meet his needs, and the mother agreed to foster placement. In his foster home, Richard achieved his ideal body weight within one year. He is no longer enuretic or encopretic. Surgery was done in early December to correct his Blount's disease.

This case fits several of the criteria that we are developing for radical therapy, namely: obesity in excess of 200% of ideal body weight; one of the more serious complications of the disease, (this child had two: Blount's disease and Pickwickian syndrome); and thirdly, failure of outpatient medical therapy.

This case illustrates the benefit of changing the environment. The child had been followed for almost two years prior to coming to us and had done nothing but gain weight. Following a change of environment and supportive but strict parenting around the issue of food, he achieved his ideal body weight.

* * * * *

—What happened to Richard's relations with his natural family after he went into the foster home?

WD: He has not seen his biologic family since then. His mother has continued to have difficulties and has not felt that she could have Richard at home with her. The remainder of Richard's family has continued to have difficulty just getting by.

—What is your hypothesis about the meaning of the overfeeding in early childhood? How does it fit into what was going on in the family, the mother's psychosis after birth and regaining of his custody shortly after. Could overfeeding be a kind of empty metaphor for nurturance, possibly even an expression of anger towards the child?

WD: We are only formulating our hypothesis about obesity in this age. Richard and the following case are both unusual in that they are

---

* A bedwetter.
† Fecal soiling, usually secondary to chronic constipation that is not of physiologic origin.

so young; we have not seen about eight cases in this age group. Each case has had rather characteristic findings. The hierarchy in these families tends to be reversed. The children tend to be autocrats, and the parents comply with their every demand. Usually there is a fair amount of friction between the parents. Often these families fit the model for potentially abusive families. I agree that in some cases the overfeeding is really a way of coping or of denying the kind of violence that these parents feel toward each other. Instead of battering, they feed.

—What is the relationship between obesity and enuresis and encopresis? You said that these disappeared as Richard's weight dropped.

WD: There are any number of studies waiting to be done on obesity in children. One of them is to look at the prevalence of encopresis and enuresis in obesity. This association was first pointed out by our nurse practitioner who also worked in the encopresis clinic who noticed that children tended to share these problems. More recent data suggests that this association may be true of severely obese children, but is not true of an unselected population.

—Do you feel that it is desirable, or required, to remove children from their family context in order to intervene successfully?

WD: Taking a child out of the home for treatment of obesity is radical therapy. I think it is justified if the major criteria that we are evolving are fulfilled. The same issues apply to removal from the home as apply to surgery for obesity. The criteria are as follows. First, a body weight in excess of 200% of ideal (there is little likelihood of spontaneous remission). This weight level has been associated with a markedly increased mortality rate in adulthood. A second criterion is the presence of one or more major complications of obesity, regardless of whether the weight criterion is fulfilled. A third criterion is a failure of optimal therapy, which to me means hypocaloric dietary therapy in good hands and family therapy. If those fail, the only two alternatives left are removal from the home or surgery. It is my feeling that removal from the home is a more conservative approach to treatment than surgery and should be tried first. Surgery is not an option for everyone but is possible for an adolescent who has almost fulfilled his/her growth potential.

—What is Richard like psychologically now? Once you lose the weight, does your psyche change accordingly?

WD: I think that is true for older children. Richard has flourished in his foster home. He is more outgoing, more relaxed, and really comfortable with his foster father with whom he comes to clinic. According to his foster father's report he is more mobile and active. As children start to lose weight they become more active and place greater demands on parents so that increased activity is often a complaint. Richard's leg surgery went off without a hitch. His gait was still the most limiting feature of his ability because he could not run. I think weight loss has been a very positive influence on him. No other neurotic symptoms have appeared.

—Richard's foster placement sounds remarkably successful. Was this hand-picked? Or were they relatives? And how did they alter the pattern so that Richard would comply with dietary restrictions and not have extraordinary behavioral difficulties?

WD: Well, in answer to your first question, we were very lucky; the chemistry was right. Foster placement may compound a problem like this. Richard was fortunate in having foster parents who were supportive and yet could put firm limits around his eating behavior. On the Psychosomatic Unit where he spent six weeks prior to his placement, limits had been set on his food intake, and the father simply continued those.

A similar case in which the mother voluntarily gave her mother the child, has had a similar kind of benefit. Young children will respond to appropriate limits on food intake. Parents may fail to set limits because they are afraid to resist, feel guilty about saying no, or fear the feelings that it brings up. In preference to becoming violent with a child or having to exert some authority, they let the child have what it wants.

—I saw Richard in consultation. You present him as the family's pet. I would like to give you another view of him. I saw him as the replacement for the absent functioning adult male in the family rather than a pet. Basically, it was a family with two females—the grandmother and the mother, the step-grandfather was alcoholic, and Richard. I saw Richard's weight gain as a way to grow up, be the big man, which is why they called him big man. That name was no accident; he was to be a man in that household. And the only way that he could be a man was to be big. And that was to eat. I would suspect that he recovered because he was allowed to be a boy. It sounds like the foster father really gives him permission to be a little boy.

WD: That raises another question—Why Richard? This family had two other boys at home. One was 17 and one was 14 or 13. Why the youngest child?

—Because you are most likely to be able to hang on to the youngest child. It could have been that the family was functioning a little bit better when those two older boys were going through their development. Frequently, for many families there is the fear that they will be left without a male in the household and there are sometimes concerted efforts made to retain a male. A very obese male child is not likely to date, marry and leave; he will be there with the family for a lifetime.

—How stable are the gains that you make? For example, when a child goes down to the ideal body weight, is ideal body weight, 50th percentile for the height? Richard's body weight seemed rather high.

WD: Richard's ideal body weight is defined as the ideal weight for height but it's a little more complicated than that because changes in frame size and muscle mass occur with obesity. In terms of long-term remissions, our success is variable. Our general success rate is low, particularly among children with massive obesity. We believe that there is a group of children who will respond no matter what you do. I think there is another group who will not respond no matter what you do. We want to identify that middle group for whom family therapy will be beneficial. Of the children who responded, a fair number have kept the weight off, maybe 60% or 70%. That includes the MIT study (Dietz and Schoeller, 1982) which involves children who are pretty highly motivated to begin with or who can already separate from their family. And that is an important distinction because there they tolerate basically two months of highly constrictive, boring, dietary therapy. Likewise, the children who are successful in the clinic are an important subgroup. We do not yet completely understand their circumstances. Nor do we understand the characteristics of those families who achieve remission and then relapse.

* * * * *

I would like to go on to the second case which I think raises some issues of interest. Theresa, an Italian girl now 6 years old, first came to the weight control program approximately 14 months ago weighing 25.1 kg, 145% of her ideal body weight with a history of obesity gradually increasing since infancy. She lives at home with her mother, father, and 3-year-old brother. Her mother has a lifelong history of obesity which resulted in gastric bypass surgery in 1980. In addition to obesity, Theresa was enuretic and a poor sleeper. The mother also mentioned that Theresa had periodic swelling of her legs associated with weight gain. This symptom was never documented. Theresa was seen by several specialty clinics; endocrine and renal evaluations were unrevealing. For approximately four months Theresa was treated with behavior modification and dietary therapy to little avail. As our treatment continued, it became apparent that the mother exercised little control over Theresa. At times she hit her because she was obese, verbally abused her and felt increasingly angry, helpless and frightened as she saw Theresa becoming as fat as she herself had been.

The father had been born and reared in rural southern Italy. The mother reported constant verbal and possible physical conflict between the parents. She described her husband as distant, stern and a harsh disciplinarian of the children. The mother had had multiple brief encounters with such services as the Child Development Clinic, the local mental health center, the psychiatry service at Beth Israel, and Children's Hospital Medical Center Outpatient Psychiatry Department. On one occasion, a referral in the emergency room was made from our clinic because of our concern that this mother was going to lose control and abuse her daughter. These interventions were usually organized around the mother, used for a short period, and then discontinued after several appointments.

In October, 1980, in collaboration with a family therapist, we offered the mother 10 sessions of family therapy. Prior to therapy we agreed that Theresa would be treated only by the weight control program, and that the father would participate in the family sessions. The family course (session by session) is summarized below.

Session One: Mother and children arrive. Larry refused to see the family because the father was not present. Mother left surprised and disappointed. This happened on at least one other occasion.

Session Two: Family arrives, children uncontrollable in the waiting room. Screaming, fighting, hitting parents, telling parents what to do and say. Family hierarchy clearly reversed with youngest child Peter who is 3, bossing Theresa who bossed the mother, who bossed the father, who withdrew. Therapeutic goal was to empower the father. Parents asked to choose behavior other than weight that they wished to change. They chose Peter's lack of toilet training, agreed to reward his successes with toys and pennies and to punish his failures with cold showers.

This family had come from southern Italy. The father's experience with child rearing came from an agrarian culture and was entirely different. The only way we could make an alliance with this father was to compromise where we could. One of the things that we could compromise around was showers. While a cold shower is not pleasant and is culturally very hard for us to see as an appropriate punishment, it was a choice of accepting cold showers or not being able to make an alliance with the father. Cold showers were used for a period of time and have now dropped out. But at that point that was the only thing on which the father and the mother could agree and agree with us.

Interestingly, the parent's technique worked in stopping Peter's enuresis. During sessions three and four, the parents spontaneously used similar techniques in handling Theresa's sleeping habits. The father began attributing the increased effectiveness in handling these previously chronic problems to being together. And in the next couple of sessions, these gains were consolidated.

Session Five: The mother and father chose to treat Theresa's enuresis. The current approach is that the father hits her. The father was given direct instructions not to hit her but to provide means for her to change her bed and pajamas. The parents were also told to limit fluids after dinner which was also a pre-diet task. Bedwetting declined but the success was diminished by differences around how to discipline. The mother tended to hit the children out of frustration and then comfort them and was consequently ineffective in changing the child's behavior. The father tended to slap with increasing intensity until the mother intervened to protect the child, thereby limiting the father's effort at discipline.

Session Six: Which was last week, started with a dramatic change. Normally we could tell when this family arrived in the clinic because the noise level in the waiting room went sky-high. This time we didn't know when the family arrived. When we came out the children were playing quietly in the waiting room, and they did not interrupt the parents during the therapy session — another dramatic change. The parents established a modified version of the father's discipline method, which the father then taught to the mother. Basically the hierarchy within the family was reestablished at this point. The discipline remained physical but was a graduated series of responses, starting with a slap on the hand, then buttocks. The parents now reward and praise the children for good behavior. The parents commented again on feeling more effective, less helpless, and more together. And the preliminary diet for Theresa was initiated.

This case again was unusual because we don't normally see children this young. There was a high potential for abuse within the family. In retrospect, I think the mother was using the complaint of her daughter's leg swelling associated with weight gain as a way of getting her into a variety of clinics. This is a very unusual complaint and in association with obesity raises all sorts of concerns about the physiologic problems associated with obesity. As I said, that problem was never documented. Nonetheless, since the parents have started therapy the mother has not gone to another clinic. That was part of the original agreement, but I think that despite the original agreement this is the kind of a family that would utilize a wide variety of different resources in the hospital. And finally, the family therapist's approach, which was to ally with the parents despite his disagreement with their methods and thereby strengthen their position in the family, made us uncomfortable in the clinic, but I think it enabled effective therapy.

* * * * *

—I was wondering about your strategy of intervention. How often do you focus on weight control as your first concern? Or, as in this case, see the weight control as initially peripheral and deal with other symptoms of family dysfunction? How do you make the decision as to how you focus in on the weight?

DB: This family was totally out of control; we didn't want to focus on food and diet, because we thought they would probably fail initially. And we didn't want them to fail on that issue. With another family, I would focus on diet earlier but not immediately because it is such a loaded issue. I spend time looking for other things before I explore diet.

WD: This child gained when she first came to the weight control program. When this happens it provokes a lot of anxiety within the clinic. While this is not characteristic it is not unusual for children to plateau while they are coming to the program.

—Gaining weight at the beginning seems surprising on one level, on another level it does not. From a psychoanalytic point of view it is like the patient who gets a little crazier at the beginning of therapy. It is the symptom that becomes a little worse at the beginning of understanding the symptom.

WD: In our clinic children have a physical exam, a dietary history, and a family assessment at the outset. At the moment we are referring for family therapy only those patients who are in critical need of it, and ultimately we hope to do a randomized clinical trial of family therapy in the treatment of disease. Involvement of other specialty medical services depend upon our findings in the physical exam.

We are now making our family therapist predict what will happen to the child in therapy, then treat the child for six to eight weeks with family therapy to see whether the predictions are fulfilled. What happens next depends on our assessment of the case. Frequently with adolescents our direction will be to try to enhance independence from the family.

—What has been the response of families when you suggest family therapy?

WD: Family therapy really starts the day that they walk in the door when we tell them that part of our treatment is the family assessment because we feel that the abuse and the course of obesity are dictated by the family constellation. People generally accept that as true. Family therapy around the issue of obesity tends to be accepted because in our clinic the focus is family and the interactional problems within the family that hinder weight loss.

More frequently now, we are putting fathers rather than mothers in charge of the diet. This has had mixed results, but there have been some cases where it has been very effective. Two-thirds of the patients that we see are girls. It is not unusual for the mothers to be overinvested in the attempts of their daughter to lose weight. The father is often distant from the issue. In order to break the maternal child dyad and alter the family interaction pattern we will involve him.

DB: In a family you have a limited number of resources. Most often one that has never been tried before is the father. It has been my experience that fathers are responsive and that mothers are relieved of a burden they have carried for years. Often, involving the father jiggles the entire family system enough to change the hierarchy.

I try grandfathers too, and grandmothers, and uncles. I look for any member of the family who could take charge of this child's diet. In one case a grandfather, limited in terms of geographical location, still has been the one who accompanies the child to the clinic and has been empowered with this child's diet.

—How do you make your decision about the family hierarchy?

DB: About who should be in charge, why are we choosing father rather than mother? In Theresa's case it is culturally consistent with their family. In a southern Italian family the male would be in charge; the mother was totally ineffective with children and was increasingly anxious about abusing them and being out of control. The father, although he punished more harshly than we could readily accept, did not lose control. It was a graduated response, one that he had obviously grown up with. It was consistently harsher and we had to scale it down, but it was never out of control.

—I would be interested to know about your formulation of the relationship of the mother to the daughter around the mother's own obviously grave history of obesity. I was interested in the possible identification between mother and daughter. Is the daughter unwittingly taking the mother's role in the marriage? What about the possibility of sexual abuse, and of enuresis being a symptom of some conflict derivative possibly over the sexualized relationship between father and daughter? For example, some of the punishments, the graduated spankings from the hand to the buttocks, the showers, may be sexualized.

DB: I know what you are saying, but for one thing the father's interest in both children was very similar. Initially, he was fairly distant, so that it wasn't until we started giving him permission to discipline the children that any of this interaction occurred. Prior to that he would just walk out of the house or just not be there. I don't think that he was around enough for the selection of punishment to fall into being a pattern of relating to the child. The relationship between the mother and the father was a problem, however.

—I'm worried about putting the father in charge of the girl's body. You know there is something about that, particularly when you have a fat Mama who is really left out in some ways then, feeling awful about her own body.

WD: I think it's important to add that we are not talking about putting fathers in charge of their adolescent girls. We are talking about fathers in charge of young children, preadolescents. And I think that often empowering a father in this respect enhances the relationship between him and his daughter, or male child for that matter.

—I think there is a deeper issue that has to do with what the family system is doing and what function obesity in parents as well as in the child serves. Since you described these marriages as frequently having a great deal of conflict between the husband and the wife, one can hypothesize that obesity in the child might serve some purpose within the marriage. One function could be to protect the child, male or female, against the father's sexual interest, given that there is a breakdown of sexual function between husband and wife. It seems that the marital relationship may need to be addressed if you want to create a family environment where it is safe for a child to be thin. Do you work in conjunction with a clinic where the parents could, in a coordinated way, be working on their own weight problems or whatever, at that time?

WD: You are right that the function of obesity may be to put distance between the parent and parent or child and parent. In fact, some of my adolescent patients have described how nice it is to have all that fat between them and the other person. You can't get close to them. And it is true that as women lose weight their marriages often dissolve because there is an interest, not necessarily sexual, in the perpetuation of obesity in one parent. We don't have a lot of experience in actually working with parents and children around diet at the same time. In our experience, the role that obesity often plays is to defuse the conflict between the parents about the obese parent's weight. In these families, failure to lose weight maintains the family's stability by avoiding open personal conflict.

DB: Empowering the father is a way of addressing the marital conflict as well as the weight problem. Most frequently the mother is ineffective in helping the child lose weight. And the father becomes angry at the mother and uses the child's continuing obesity as proof of the mother's ineffectiveness. By empowering the father, you exclude this area from the marital conflict. But the broader marital conflict often does not get dealt with. These are families for whom a referral must be made elsewhere.

—It has been mentioned that two-thirds of the patients are girls. Do you think that is because girls are more likely to be obese, or that culturally there is more concern about obesity in girls? And in the fathers and mothers that you see, is it usually the mother who has the overweight problem as opposed to the father?

WD: The patients who come to our clinic are not a true reflection of the prevalence of the disease in the population. In fact, the prevalence of obesity in boys is the same as it is in girls, although there are some socioeconomic differences. The risk of a child's being obese is the same whether the obese parent is a mother or a father. We have observed no consistent pattern of parental obesity.

—Are there any factors that enable you to predict how well the child responds to treatment? Who would you see as an ideal family for an effective weight loss program, ie, gradual vs recent onset; cognitive vs chronological level of the child; intact nonintact family?

WD: That question is the area of our most intense interest. The children who do well generally have families in which they are seen as separate individuals. Giving responsibility to them is not simply verbal but an actual empowering of the child to lose weight. I don't think age at onset or duration of obesity has anything to do with success nor does the apparent causal event. The children who do best are children whose parents are lean and are married rather than divorced or separated (Dietz, 1983). But I am not sure of the behavioral mechanisms responsible for those two correlates.

DB: There are two groups of families that I can identify as ones in which the children would lose weight. In one, the child is under 11-years-old and during family assessment, with both parents there, I can demonstrate that the parents can control this child without feeling either guilt or ambivalence. In the second group the child is older, somewhere around the age of 15. Usually there is a problem in the marital relationship and the child may have spent years being entrapped in a relationship with one or both parents; but the child is bright and able intellectually to separate the diet from all the other things going on his life.

WD: The third category where our greatest success lies is with very young children with the pattern that I described earlier. At the moment, our success rate among that group is 50% to 60% which is considerably higher than it is among other groups.

As Theresa's case demonstrates, intervention that alters a pattern by working with families often has potential for success. Young children are the easiest group with whom to deal. More difficult are the cases that we see all the time—11 or 12 year olds who have been obese for five years and for whom we do not have a good history of onset. Whatever the factors were that precipitated the disease may no longer be active in perpetuating it. It would be premature to do more than speculate about what is happening in those families. Our goal is to learn that and to be successful in altering that.

—Other than these cases, how much do you see the obese child as the victim of physical abuse?

WD: I think these are exceptional cases, and I do not really see the child as victim. I see the child as tied up in a system which has them obese. The mean percent ideal body weight in our clinic is 165%. We see, I would say, 5% or 10% who are over 200% of their ideal body weight. Within that 200% group, I would say that the majority have an abusive type family situation—not latent physical abuse but a chaotic disorganized family in desperate need of intervention.

—Do you report abuse and neglect in such families?

WD: We have done so on occasion. I make it quite clear at the outset that the family has a major problem, and I outline the complications for them and tell them what the course of the disease is likely to be, and tell them that if children are unable to lose weight at home that I will alter the environment in order to protect their health. If all that fails, then their only recourse is surgery or foster care. I do not think that reporting abuse or neglect is a good way of establishing alliance with a family and helping the child. After all, they come to me because of their concern about an obese child. In several cases I have been able to convince the family to opt for voluntary placement based on that alliance. I point out to them that I share their concern about their child's obesity, and that it is clear that the child is not losing weight at home. Don't they think that the next step is really to try that child in another

96

environment? That has worked. However, if I am unable to convince a family with a massively obese child that they must respond to that problem, I do not hesitate to file.

—What are your feelings about the relationship between obesity and anorexia nervosa?

WD: I think obesity is the other side of the anorexia coin. If you compare the prevalence of anorexia with socioeconomic status and obesity, the curves are basically reciprocal. The prevalence of anorexia nervosa rises among girls as you go upward in socioeconomic classes and obesity falls. I think that the family patterns are often similar. Characteristically, anorexia families tend to have an overenmeshment of the parent with the child. Why starvation rather than obesity is chosen, I am not sure. There are reports of people who successfully resolve their anorexia only to become obese, and vice versa. I have not seen those cases. But certainly, bulimorrexia, the gorging and vomiting syndrome, indicates marked ambivalence about eating. Therefore, it is not surprising that there is that crossover.

BIBLIOGRAPHY

Dietz WH: Obesity in infants, children and adolescents in the United States. I. Identification, natural history and after effects. *Nutr Res* 1981;1:117-137.

Dietz WH: Obesity in infants, children and adolescents in the United States. II. Causality. *Nutr Res* 1981;1:193-208.

Dietz WH: Childhood obesity: susceptibility, cause, and management. *J Pediatr* 1983;103:676-686.

Dietz WH Jr: Family characteristics affect rates of weight loss in obese children. *Nutr Res* 1983;3:43-50.

Dietz WH, Schoeller DA: Optimal therapy for obese adolescents: Comparison of protein plus glucose and protein plus fat. *J Pediatr* 1982;100:636-644.

Hoffman L: *Foundations of Family Therapy*. New York, Basic Books Inc, 1981.

Minuchin S, Rosman BL, Baker L: *Psychosomatic Families*. Cambridge, Harvard University Press, 1978.

CHAPTER 10

Pediatric Assessment and Differential Diagnosis of Child Abuse

Daniel B. Kessler

I want to start with a brief historical background on the definition of child abuse. While it is true that child abuse has existed for a long time, as long as there have been children and adults, during the first half of this century society appeared to deny that such behavior was possible.

Pediatric radiologists played the principal role in the recent rediscovery that children may be abused by those charged with their care. For this reason the early reports on child abuse laid heavy stress on radiological aspects. It was Caffey, a pediatric radiologist at Baby's Hospital in New York, who in 1946 first hinted at the traumatic nature of injuries to children suffered at the hands of their caretakers when he demonstrated the association of multiple fractures of the long bones in six infants with chronic subdural hematomas (blood clots on the surface of the brain). Notwithstanding the general acceptance that most, if not all subdural hematomas were caused by trauma, Caffey noted, "the history of trauma is lacking in almost one-half of the cases." And that is still true today. Similarly he noted, "the injuries which caused the fractures in the long bones of these patients, were either not observed or were denied when observed." He explained this by the following statement:

> The negative history of trauma in so many cases can probably be best explained by assuming that sometimes lay observers do not properly evaluate ordinary but causally significant accidents, especially falls on the head, and that other important traumatic episodes pass unnoticed or are forgotten by the time delayed cranial symptoms appear. Also, recognized injuries may be denied by mothers and nurses because injury to an infant implies negligence on the part of the caretaker.

And this is still true today. Though he couched his suspicions in the softest of terms when one reads his paper again today, it seems clear what Caffey must have been thinking. He made the following additional observations:

In each case, unexplained fresh fractures appeared shortly after the patient had arrived home after discharge from the hospital. In one of these cases the infant was clearly unwanted by both parents. And this raised the question of intentional ill treatment of the infant. The evidence was inadequate to prove or disprove the point.

The traumatic nature of these injuries in infants and young children, which prior to Caffey were explained as some pathologic fragility of the bone, were soon revealed by other radiologists for what they were. In 1953 Frederick Silverman, a student of Caffey's, clearly implicated the parents or guardian as a cause of a particular type of skeletal trauma in children, and he described the radiologic features. Then in 1962, Kempe, Silverman and their colleagues wakened the medical profession with their coining of the term *the battered child syndrome.* And they discussed unrecognized trauma in children in a way which left no doubt as to the mechanism of these injuries.

In two years, the first state law on child abuse was passed. By 1968, all states had such laws. Today the definition of child abuse has been much expanded to include neglect, emotional injury or deprivation, and sexual abuse as well as physical injury. There are those who would broaden the scope of the definition even further. Gil has defined child abuse as any action which interferes with the child's achievement of physical and psychological potential. Parenthetically, however, there is also a move underway to further restrict the definition of child abuse. Representative of such a stance are the views expressed by the Juvenile Justice Standards Project and the report of the Carnegie Commission on Children. Both would tend to define abuse more narrowly and restrict judicial discretion when dealing with it. So we see that the definition of child abuse developed from a rather narrow radiological diagnosis of severe injury to the definition in common use today, and we also see some of the forces acting to change that definition.

It is important to note that in current pediatric practice child abuse is recognized as a symptom of broader family distress, and the discovery of abuse should open the door to help for the entire family, which is often a family in crisis. The goals of assessment are threefold: to assess the stresses on the family, to determine the ongoing risk to the child, and to begin the helping process. The medical evaluation is only part of the larger assessment.

The ability to differentiate between accidental or inflicted injury may prevent the tragedy of the abused child being sent home to be seriously reinjured. Among the physical findings of nonaccidental trauma, abnormalities of the skin are among the most common and easily recognized. Over 90% of child abuse cases have skin findings such as bruises and burns.

Important in the differentiation of inflicted or nonaccidental trauma from accidental injury is the location and pattern of the injury.

BRUISES

We will first consider bruises. Certain sites are so common for inflicted injury that bruises in these locations are almost diagnostic. Bruises on the buttocks and lower back are almost always related to punishment. Corporal punishment of children in the name of discipline is an accepted practice in our society. The question is often asked where discipline ends and abuse begins. One practical answer may be when it leaves bruises or other signs of injury.

Genital injuries are also often inflicted. A pinch mark on the glans of the penis looks like two small crescent shaped marks facing each other. Bruises that are found in the genital area or inner thighs may be inflicted for toileting problems. Injuries in this area should also raise the question of sexual abuse.

Bruises on the face, especially of the cheek or earlobe, are usually due to being slapped or cuffed. When very recent, the finger outlines are often visible. Or they can be more subtle and several parallel lines that run through a fading bruise may be seen. Injury to the ear can be sustained either by pulling at it or by cuffing. A child may be pinched on the earlobe and pulled. When children are slapped in this location you can often see multiple pinpoint bleeding spots in the skin called petechiae. Injuries to the mouth are uncommon in truly accidental trauma. They often occur from forced feeding or forcing a pacifier into the mouth of a screaming child in an attempt to quiet him. Such an injury may include, for example, bruises on the cheeks and below the chin that cannot be self-inflicted until a child is able to sit unaided and then inadvertently fall forward.

Some injuries will remain hidden unless they are looked for. Bruises to the neck are almost always inflicted and are due to being choked or strangled. This may involve the human hands, in which case finger impressions may be evident, or marks from a rope or cord. Tie marks on a child's ankles or wrists are also diagnostic of inflicted injury. Depending upon the material used, the nature of the injury will vary. A rope or narrow cord can cause narrow groove marks, a strap or piece of sheet material tied around an ankle can cause a friction burn and blisters to form around the ankle, but being somewhat wider than a rope it may not cut as deeply into the skin. Abrasions that run from each corner of the mouth may be caused by a gag. The intent may be to keep a child from screaming. Thus, the location of an injury can be extremely helpful in determining its nature.

Bruises have some characteristic patterns. The human hands may leave an outline because only the capillaries at the edges of the injury are stretched enough to rupture. Grabbing or squeezing and forcibly holding may leave oval-shaped pressure bruises which are actually fingerprints. Human hand prints can be recognized by finger joints or ends of fingers even when some of the impression of the hand may be missing. One must use a bit of imagination when looking at these types of injuries.

Human bite marks are distinctive. They are paired crescent-shaped bruises that contain individual teeth marks. Bite marks may be blamed on a sibling. Simple measurements can distinguish between the bite marks left by primary teeth, such as in a youngster of less than 6 or 8 years of age, and bite marks left by the permanent teeth of an adult.

Marks or bruises caused by other objects can also leave distinctive impressions. Strap marks cause linear bruises one to two inches in width and often cover a curved body surface. Distinguishing features such as eyelets, outlines of buckles, or the tongue or tapered area of the end of the belt can sometimes be identified. Loop marks on the skin may come from being struck with a doubled over lamp cord or rope. They, too, are diagnostic. Multiple bruises are also extremely diagnostic of multiple beatings. Bizarre shaped bruises may be inflicted by unusual items. One child was hit with tiny railroad tracks from a toy train set, and they showed the obvious pattern of the railroad track.

Aging of Bruises

Skin evidence can sometimes be ambiguous. Mongolian spots are often mistaken for bruises. They are often present at birth on dark colored skin, last approximately two to three years, are generally reddish blue, do not change color and have clear-cut margins. Bruises, on the other hand, go through distinct color changes. Physicians are commonly asked to date bruises. If a bruise is still swollen and tender it is usually fresh and always less than two days old. In the first five days, the bruise is red, blue or purple, and as the hemoglobin pigment of the blood deposited in the skin is broken down, the bruise will usually go through three distinct color changes caused by the breakdown of the heme pigment which begins at the periphery of the bruise.

The first change in color is to green and occurs in a minimum of five days. Within a few days after this the color will change to yellow. In a few more days the bruise will take on a brownish discoloration. This brown color may persist from a few days to two weeks before the bruise finally clears.

When evaluating bruises it is important to keep in mind the fact that all children bruise. Certain bruising is common and normal. Young babies will commonly scratch themselves in the cheek, ear, nose and eyes.

This is usually due to long fingernails and will disappear once the nails are trimmed. The most common site of multiple benign bruising in childhood is on the knee and shin area. Forehead bruises are frequent findings in toddlers. When children get other bruises from falling they are usually circular, nondescript in pattern, involve bony prominences such as the chin or elbow, and occur on just one body surface or plain. Bruises on multiple body planes are usually inflicted. Nondescript bruises become suspicious of abuse when they occur on soft parts of the body such as the cheek, the fleshy part of the arm, buttocks, and abdominal wall.

* * * * *

—We sometimes hear that a child bruises easily. What does that mean?

DK: When a child is brought into the emergency room you are often told that the child bruises easily. The nature and location of the bruises might make it clear that they are from inflicted injuries rather than normal accidents. One thing to be aware of is that such bruises will usually continue to occur in a hospital setting when a child is being observed. If the bruises do not seem to accumulate further under such observation, those bruises and the history of easy bruising has to be questioned. A number of laboratory tests can be done to screen for underlying bleeding disorders.

—You may have capillary fragility with children who are malnourished, especially with vitamin C deficiency as you might see with infants who fail to thrive or who are severely neglected. Vitamin C depletes very quickly. This is important because there may be no true physical abuse in, for instance, a failure to thrive child who may yet have a tendency to bruise.

* * * * *

BURNS

I want to turn next to burns. About 10% of physical abuse cases involve burns. It is always somewhat more problematic for me when an abuse case involves burns.

To me, purposely inflicting a burn on a child suggests a bit more pathology. The most commonly inflicted burn seen in the office setting are those caused by lit cigarettes. Smaller but similar burns have also been caused by incense and match tips. They are all characteristic. They are circular in shape, punched out in appearance, and similar in size. The only differential point to be considered is that of a condition called **bullous impetigo,** which is caused by the staph bacteria. This usually involves lesions of various sizes that occur in groups and usually have signs of pus present; they will increase in number while the child is in the hospital under observation. It should be noted that bumping into a cigarette should cause only a single burn.

Four distinct patterns of inflicted burns have been described. Forced immersion burns yield a donut-shaped distribution of burn with the spared area frequently on the buttocks or back. The unburned skin, shaped like a donut hole, may have been forcibly held against the container or tub and therefore spared any prolonged contact with the hot water. Because the container is cooler than the water which has just been poured in it, it transfers less heat to the skin. Such burns involving the buttocks and genital/rectal area are almost always inflicted as punishment for bedwetting or bowel training problems, or may be due to an older sibling trying to give his younger brother or sister a bath and only turning on the hot water tap. (This may be viewed as an accident secondary to failure to supervise or protect young children.)

A splash burn may produce nonuniform, multiple noncontiguous burn areas sometimes with arrowhead patterns. If a child's body is immersed in a maximally flexed position, the skin folds of the chest may be spared and a striped pattern will result.

A forced immersion burn of a leg may produce a burn well above the ankle level with no spash marks. Children are not foolish enough to place an extremity into hot water to any depth, so burns with a glove or stocking distribution should always be considered inflicted.

A burn caused by contact with a hot object is called a dry contact burn. It usually involves only one surface of the body. The shape of the burn sometimes can be diagnostic, such as when a child is forcibly held against a heating grate, touched with a hot iron, or forced to sit on an electric hotplate. The child who falls against a radiator or another hot object will not stay there long. The pain on contact would usually cause a retraction to remove the body part and only when it is forcibly held will such an extensive burn result.

HEAD INJURIES

Head injuries are primarily subdural hematomas (blood clots on the surface of the brain) and are the most serious of inflicted injuries. One study suggests that approximately 25% of children with subdural hematomas die, and a majority of the survivors are left with mental retardation, blindness, cerebral palsy, and seizures. These children often show irritability, vomiting, a decreased level of consciousness, breathing difficulties, apnea (the absence of respiration), or convulsions. Often the child also has skull fractures.

While it is common for striking of the skull to result in injuries on both sides of the brain from a coup contra-coup mechanism (the brain shaking around in the cranial skeleton), in order to break the bone on both sides, both sides have to be hit. So a story that the child fell and hit the side of the head on the sink does not agree with the findings of multiple skull fractures involving both sides. But a single trauma can cause a long and continous fracture that extends around the skull.

Sutures are points at which the different bone segments in the skull come together. They usually mesh together by a certain age. If there is increased intracranial pressure caused by the presence of subdurals, suture lines may be widely split. This is a common finding in these kinds of head injuries.

Retinal hemorrhages (bleeding spots at the back of the eye) also help to make the diagnosis. The optic nerve is a white disc with blood vessels that course from it in the back of the retina. Circular areas of hemorrhage are usually present in cases of subdural hematoma. A physician will take a look at the retina (the back of the eye) using an ophthalmoscope; different lenses allow focusing at the right distance behind the cornea (the front of the eye). This often requires a good deal of skill with children. One reason is that they are not usually cooperating, and a second is that the pupil (the opening of the eye that constricts and expands according to the amount of light that impinges on it) is usually more reactive in children. It very often requires an experienced neurologist or ophthalmologist who might have to use a medication to dilate the eye and then look at the back.

BONE INJURIES

Over 20% of physically abused children have some x-ray evidence of bone trauma, and some will have overt fractures. Spiral fractures involving the humorous or the upper arm bone are often thought to be diagnostic of twisting injuries; however, it should be borne in mind that once the child is able to stand and walk, spiral fractures of the femur (the upper leg bone) or the tibia (the lower leg bone) may also occur. These fractures are usually accidental. One of the classic early findings on an x-ray is a chip fracture or corner fracture. The normally smooth contour of the bone is disrupted and a chip of bone is torn off. This may also be called an avulsion fracture which is a tearing away of a part of the bone that is usually attached to a tendon or ligament. The corner of the metaphysis, the widened portion of the long bone, is usually torn off during wrenching or twisting injuries which may occur when the legs of an infant are forcibly and suddenly spread as during a diaper change. The chip fracture is visible on x-ray, immediately after the injury.

Other signs of bony trauma, however, may not be immediately visible. The periosteum (covering of the bone) may also be torn off, but the periosteal reaction will not be visible until it has calcified. This process takes about 10 to 14 days. Then an x-ray will show some double contour lines around the bone. Normally the surface is smooth and some tissue density is seen; darkened or more white area on the x-ray indicate that calcification is present in the tissues immediately surrounding the bone. At four to six weeks after an injury, the subperiosteal calcification will become solid and then begin to smooth out and remodel.

Bone Scanning

Because subtle degrees of bone trauma will not be visible on plain radiographs until the subperiosteal hematoma calcifies, which takes 10 to 14 days, such a site has to be reexamined in two weeks time. One problem is that frequently the child is sent home when the x-ray is negative and not asked to come back for reexamination and is then lost to follow up. Newer techniques now make it possible to diagnose early bone trauma more easily. Such a technique is bone scanning. Bone scanning is a diagnostic procedure that uses radioactively labeled phosphate compounds which preferentially seek out and are incorporated into areas of increased metabolic activity. These bone seeking radionuclides allow us to picture on gamma counting equipment sites of early bone trauma. The very beginning of some subperiosteal reaction can be seen. This is in about five to seven days. A fuzzy outline of the bones with an increased uptake in areas of rapid metabolic turnover can be seen. Such a technique is used to show early signs of infection and also some bone tumors and is now being increasingly used in traumatic injuries as well.

One advantage of this technique is that the entire skeleton can be imaged at one time without additional patient radiation. Individual x-rays of each of the bones are not taken. It involves one injection and then simply the scanning using the gamma counting devices that scan the entire skeleton, either of specific sites or of the entire skeleton. Also, it makes it more easy to visualize some difficult areas, such as the vertebral column. And within 24 hours, bone scanning techniques will show increased uptake in occult fractures of the ribs, hairline fractures of the long bones and compression fractures such as might be present in vertebral bodies. This makes it easier to have indications of early trauma before signs are visible on the plain radiographs.

* * * * *

—With the bone scan, do you have to give radiation doses that would be detrimental to the youngster?

DK: No, not at all. Newer compounds have a much shorter half-life and therefore the actual dose to the tissues is minimal. In fact the dosage is about one-half to one-quarter the dosage in ordinary x-rays. That is a little different in much smaller babies in which it depends on body surface area. And the radiation dose to the gonadal tissue is less than it would be in a conventional x-ray.

—Why is there often a decision made about long bone x-rays versus bone scans and why do people say that they do not think a bone scan is necessary? We run into this all the time.

DK: In most centers a complete skeletal survey consists of the following: skull films, a number of views that might include a frontal view, straight on, a lateral view, and also a Towne view which attempts to demonstrate the bones of the face and orbits without obstruction by some of the thicker bones of the skull that usually get in the way in the other two views. It involves a chest film to show the heart, lungs, clavicle, shoulders and ribs. It will involve films which will be lateral views of the spine in the area of the neck and upper, middle, and lower torso, and also films of the upper and lower limbs. And this will include the pelvis, hands, feet, and any other additional x-rays that might be indicated by the nature of the injury. A bone survey will show a definite fracture immediately. A plain radiograph will show a definite fracture immediately.

However, where there are more occult or more subtle injuries, those changes won't be shown for seven to 10 days. A bone scan should ideally be done within 48 hours of the injury to show the changes that it picks up. It is very sensitive to changes within metabolic rate. That is usually within 24 to 48 hours.

When there is a long delay, say a week, some people feel that a bone scan would not be better than a regular x-ray, because at that point, they believe the changes should be visible on a plain radiograph. In the period between the incident and up to a week, valuable additional information can probably still be obtained by a bone scan and it should be considered.

—You might miss a growth plate fracture with just a bone scan since it is already very hct. Probably both an x-ray and a bone scan are necessary.

DK: Bone scans have a relatively grainy appearance and are not very good in terms of anatomic detail. What they give you is a sense of function. You are measuring metabolic activity and enhanced metabolic activity in the sites of trauma. A plain radiograph will certainly give you more information about actual structure.

When an x-ray demonstrates bone injuries in different stages of healing, it is representative of repeated assault and is therefore diagnostic of child abuse.

—What is a green stick fracture?

DK: If you have taken a stick in your walks in the woods and broken it, and if it is a fresh twig not completely dried out, it may break on only one surface—the convex surface, not the concave surface. An incomplete fracture that usually occurs from a bending or breaking action and only involves the convex surface is called a green stick fracture.

—Considering a complete break as opposed to a break on one side, is one more diagnostic of inflicted injury than the other?

DK: It would depend on the circumstances like the location, and on whether the history given is consistent with the injury.

* * * * *

OTHER PHYSICAL SYMPTOMS

There are many other manifestations of child abuse. Inflicted abdominal injuries are the second most common cause of death in battered children. And this is usually due to shock—the shock state that can result from bleeding. These injuries are usually caused by a punch or a kick that compresses the abdominal organ, be it the intestine, the liver, the spleen, or the pancreas against the anterior spinal column which is a very rigid structure. Child abuse should be considered in any unexplained abdominal injury. Because the skin over the abdomen is so easily distensible, a major injury to an abdominal organ may exist without any sign of trauma to the overlying skin. This brings us to information obtained on a review of the history.

When presented with a traumatic injury one must obtain a certain miminum amount of information. This includes when the injury occurred. Was it in the early morning hours? Was there a delay in seeking medical care? How did the injury occur? What was the sequence of events? Is there a discrepancy between the history and the physical findings? Who was with the child at the time of the injury? Did that person accompany the child to the medical facility? Certain injury histories are diagnostic, or at least extremely suspicious of physical abuse or nonaccidental trauma. When a child readily indicates that a particular adult hurt him, it is almost always true. A confession of either parent with a report of an eye witness are also diagnostic but seldom available. When one parent accuses another parent, it is usually accurate if they are not involved in a custody dispute. An unexplained or spontaneous injury is always suspicious. Parents of victims of innocent injuries often know to the minute where and when their child was hurt. They also show complete willingness to discuss it in detail.

Sometimes a parent will offer an explanation of a given injury that is implausible or inconsistent with either common sense or medical judgment. Sometimes a minor accident is described but the injuries are major and multiple in number. Or the behavior described that led to the accident is impossible at the child's level of development, for example, when it is claimed that a 10-month-old child climbed into a tub and turned on the hot water thereby scalding himself. Parents may make their explanations implausible by repeatedly changing them. Self-inflicted injury is unlikely; children rarely deliberately injure themselves, and for small babies this explanation is usually absurd. In general the child who isn't crawling yet is unable to cause an injury to himself; fractures in children under the age of 1 year are almost uniformly inflicted. When parents have a difficulty coming up with an explanation of an injury they commonly project the blame on rough play with the sibling. In the approximately 1% of injuries in which the sibling is responsible, reporting is probably appropriate anyway as part of the effort to prevent recurrences. Other parties may frequently be blamed, such as the neighbor or the baby-sitter, and this always requires further investigation.

Parents often come in immediately when their child is injured. In contrast, some abused children are not brought in for a considerable period of time despite major injury. An extreme situation is when the child is brought in nearly dead. The time of the occurrence may be significant. Accidents occurring between midnight and six AM are always suspicious.

* * * * *

—I don't think you can make absolute statements like, "Parents of victims of innocent injuries will show complete willingness to discuss every detail of an injury." People feel guilty. Although they may not have inflicted it, they think, "Oh my God, I shouldn't have let Johnny go out to play." You really have to be sensitive to individuals.

DK: In the emergency room when perhaps the physician dealing with the youngster is not a pediatrician and not familiar with childhood accidents, the tendency may be to let these injuries go. I think that it is important to develop a healthy respect for the different possibilities. You do have to temper that with respect for individual differences and for people, but the intent here is to sensitize people to be suspicious, to sensitize physicians to what they should look for.

—But is it sensitizing people to be human, to hear what people have to say and to evaluate it in a sensitive way? I am concerned about going overboard on the other side.

DK: You know that I agree with you. What I am presenting here is somewhat limited because I am presenting medical fact. The medical assessment is only one part of it. My tendency is to perhaps over-diagnose, given the dangers implicit in sending a very young child home when the injury is an inflicted one. These injuries will often recur and perhaps be more serious the next time. So my tendency is to lean over backwards the other way, at least at this demonstration.

—One of the things that we are getting from people is stark fear about being labeled as abusive parents. Certainly many people are, in fact, holding back and sometimes worry about even bringing in a child with an injury. This is true of parents who have not in any sense been labeled as child abusers. There is a terrible fear about society's view at this moment.

DK: What I meant to imply is that when you are presented with these types of injuries and an ambiguous situation you have to consider the possibility of child abuse and then evaluate it in the larger context. Other sources of information are the child's interaction with his parents, the relevance of some of the historical facts, the search for some other perhaps concrete signs, and the opinions of other professionals involved. The suspicion should lead one to look deeper and not to ignore one's gut feelings.

—I think the primary thing is that one is really looking at the best interests of the child to protect the child. It is important to be alert about the possibilities. And hopefully when one approaches the parents it is not in an accusatory way but in a supportive way, and in a way that makes it clear that the goal is to help, which is the missing piece of this.

DK: In closing I have one statement to make. The physical manifestations of child abuse that I have tried to demonstrate here often speak for children who cannot speak for themselves. I think their value cannot be underestimated.

BIBLIOGRAPHY

Ayoub C, Pfelfer D: Burns as a manifestation of child abuse and neglect. *Am J Dis Child* 1979;133:910-914.

Bittner S, Newberger EH: Pediatric understanding of child abuse and neglect. *Pediatr Rev* 1981;2:197-207.

Caffey J: Multiple fractures in the long bones of infants suffering from chronic subdural hematoma. *Am J Roentgenol* 1946;56:163-173.

Caffey J: The whiplash shaken infant syndrome. *Pediatr* 1974;54:396.

Cohn AH: The pediatrician's role in the treatment of child abuse: Implications from a national evaluation study. *Pediatr* 1980;65:358-360.

Ellerstein NS: The cutaneous manifestations of child abuse and neglect. *Am J Dis Child* 1979;133:906-909.

Gil D: *Violence Against Children: Physical Child Abuse in the United States*. Cambridge, Mass, Harvard University Press, 1970.

Kempe CH, Silverman FH, Steele BF, et al: The battered child syndrome. *JAMA* 1962;181:17-24.

Pascoe JM, Hildebrandt HM, et al: Patterns of skin injury in nonaccidental and accidental injury. *Pediatr* 1979;64:245-247.

Silverman FH: The roentgen manifestations of unrecognized skeletal trauma in infants. *Am J Roetgenol* 1953;69:413.

Wilkinson RW: Imaging of the abused child, in Newberger EH (ed): *Child Abuse*. Boston, Mass, Little, Brown, 1982.

CHAPTER 11

Psychiatric Issues and the Physician's Role in Reporting Child Abuse

Herschel D. Rosenzweig

It's not nearly as remarkable that so much child abuse has been recognized in the past two decades since Kempe's landmark work and exposé of the issue as it is that so little had been reported by humane and concerned practitioners during the decades and centuries earlier.

Why have physicians failed to report child abuse in earlier periods? For one, it has been a time-honored tradition to assume both that parents know what is best for their children and that parents always have their children's best interest at heart. Secondly, it has been well documented that children have long been considered the property of their parents and the notion that youngsters have independent feelings, let alone rights, is historically a relatively new concept.

Even in modern times, however, when we are attuned to the rights and needs of children and the potential ambivalence of parents, the recognition and reporting of child abuse continues to be obscured. In order for physicians to recognize and report child abuse, they may need to understand the dynamics that make these tasks so difficult.

The scene that first confronts a doctor when an injured child is brought in is one that may seem quite inconsistent with child abuse: a concerned anxious parent and a child clearly more trusting of the parent than of the physician. A child, unlike an adult, is brought to the physician for care by someone other than himself. When the physician is a stranger to the child, the child often experiences anxiety in his presence, especially when the youngster knows that doctors are sometimes obliged to inflict pain in the process of their work to relieve it. Consequently, the child may cling to his or her parents who are now acting under the loving, caring side of their ambivalence even though they may have been more affected by the angry, resentful side when they inflict injury.

When the physician is not a stranger to the family, his familiarity is often based on long-term contact with parents who have brought their children for well-baby checkups and immunizations. It is often difficult for the family physician to recognize or even suspect that these same caring, concerned parents could have been directly responsible for their child's current pain. When such parents are expressing great anxiety about a child's well being it seems presumptuous or even cynical to wonder whether their anxiety is evoked as much out of guilt or fear of repercussion for having inflicted the injury as out of anxiety about the child's welfare.

Even when the physician does recognize the possibility of child abuse, many factors make it extremely difficult for him to pursue his suspicion with the child's parents.

The physician is often, by temperament and training, prone to be compassionate. It is clearly the physician's duty to diagnose and treat disease, to comfort and instruct patients, and to support, educate and reassure families. It is not so clearly the physician's duty to appear to accuse. Physicians often have difficulty confronting patients with unhappy news. When the news is that the physician cannot accept the parent's account of how injury has occurred and if he believes that the parent, either by neglect or by intent, may be at least partially responsible for the injury, the physician may have great difficulty bearing such a message.

Trust and Confrontation

Mutual trust is an important prerequisite in the relationship between the physician and the family he treats. The family continues the relationship because the members have confidence in their doctor. They trust his judgement, trust him or her to respect the confidentiality of their communications and trust the physician to protect their best interest. The physician, in turn, trusts that the family will be forthright and honest in the information they give him in order to diagnose and treat them to the best of his ability. When the family physician begins to suspect that he is dealing with an abusive situation which has not been acknowledged by the parents, that bond of trust is strained. Confrontation of the family with his concerns may stress the relationship intolerably and the need to report his suspicions to an outside investigator may disrupt it entirely. Such a consequence is not only highly distasteful to most physicians but also engenders great anxiety as they may have reason to believe that once a family's ability to place its trust in him has been shaken, it can never be reestablished. In order to preserve that delicate bond of trust the physician is often tempted to try to manage a case of suspected child abuse without formally labeling even in his own mind. This denial may be rationalized as being in the service of assuring continuity of care to the child and the family or by fear that in reporting his suspicions he may terrify the family and drive them away from any source of potential help. The physician may fear that if his suspicions are wrong the family whose caretaking capacity he has doubted will not appreciate his concern. They may not only leave his practice but also jeopardize his relationship with other families. Physicians sometimes imagine being assaulted by indignant parents or being sued for their good intentions.

The physician may fear that if he is correct in his presumptive diagnosis, the parents may not only leave his practice but the area altogether. They may avoid seeking further medical aid from any source. In reality, frequent moves characterize the life of many abusive families. Discontinuity of medical care is a common occurrence even without reporting. The justifiably apprehensive physician may also fear that the vulnerable child might be further mistreated for seeming to have created a situation in which the parents feel put in jeopardy.

Control of the Case

Reluctance to recognize child abuse and thereby oblige oneself to report it in accordance with current legislation may also emanate from the physician's fear of losing control of the case and his reluctance to transfer the primary care responsibility to others whom he or she may not know and may trust less than the family in question.

Physicians tend to be extremely reluctant to submit reports which will involve them and the parents with an agency of the state. Most physicians in our society have long had deep-rooted apprehensions about the intrusion of government agencies into the practice of medicine and into the sanctity of family life.

Moreover, many physicians have serious doubts about the competency of the state's social service personnel to offer troubled families real assistance in coping with their preexisting problems, let alone the crisis which may be created by the report which he is mandated to make if he recognizes an abusive situation. Many physicians' only contact with state agencies — dealing with Medicaid and Medicare — results in long delays and red tape. Their knowledge of protective service agencies may come mainly from the usually unhappy endings and mismanaged cases which are reported in the media. Consequently, many practitioners have little hope of finding dedicated, well trained and sensitive specialists to respond effectively to a report he is obliged to submit if he recognizes a case of suspected abuse. Unfortunately the general impression that protective social workers are overworked, undersupervised, underpaid, overly stressed and highly subject to professional burnout is probably not exaggerated, but the notion that such workers are generally insensitive and uncaring is truly a misrepresentation.

Whatever the reason for potential mismanagement, however, the physician who has made an emotional and professional commitment to a family is often reticent to entrust his patients to an uncertain fate over which he may feel little influence. He may anticipate that reporting his suspicions may subject the family, which already has more problems than it can handle, to a scenario of institutional abuse rather than genuine assistance.

Fear of Court

Most pediatricians and family physicians are also apprehensive about being drawn into the unfamiliar world of the courtroom. They anticipate that if they report their suspicions of child abuse, they are opening a legalistic Pandora's box — a difficulty for their patients as well as for themselves. Although expert in their skills, many physicians become quite anxious about the prospect of having to go to court, long waits and delays, loss of time from one's practice, and the potential indignity of attack upon one's credentials and judgment. The physician may fear that by going to court he will lose not only one family but time for serving others as well.

It is often difficult to make a major decision which may have serious sequelae in the face of uncertainty even if based on strong suggestive evidence or high probability. In medicine it is often appropriate to be cautious, to take a wait and see approach, to assume that with the passage of time and events the truth of the situation will emerge with greater clarity. While this is often a reasonable attitude and diagnostic tactic, in cases of child abuse the consequences of delay may be irreversible damage to a child. By the time that evidence becomes clearer, the results may be tragic. While the physician may not be able to define the source of the child's distress with certainty, he can define the most probable cause of presenting problems in order to ensure that the child will not suffer further injury.

Once a physician is convinced that he must act, his anxiety about confronting the child's family may impel him to avoid raising the issue with them directly but to implore someone else, such as the social worker or the most available trauma team to report his concern to the public agency empowered to investigate abuse. While this division of labor may seem more comfortable and efficient, such an approach may be seen as evasive and deceptive to the parents — a persecutory allegation, rather than an effort to obtain supportive and protective service for the entire family as well as the injured child. Much trust and potential support is lost if the physician does not approach the parents himself.

Effective Communication and Professional Work

There is no way of guaranteeing that any of the fears mentioned will not prove justified. However, it is possible for a physician to communicate his suspicions and concerns to a family in a manner which may facilitate the family's responsiveness rather than to provoke a negative reaction. Even in cases of recurrent abuse, it is a rare family indeed in which there is not a positive side to the family's ambivalence, a side that seeks to protect the child from neglect and abuse. Even though this relatively positive aspect of abusive parents may be ineffectual it may be sufficiently potent to impel them to get the child to medical attention initially.

First, the physician must recognize the following paradox about his inclinations vis a vis the parents' needs. When allegedly accidental injuries are observed in a child brought to medical attention by an over-anxious or guilt-ridden parent, the physician may perceive it as his humanitarian duty to reassure and relieve the parent's guilt. Consequently, the physician may be reluctant to probe deeper or to suggest doubt or cast suspicion upon the parent's veracity as well as their caretaking abilities. For the parent whose negative feelings toward the child have overwhelmed him, whose control over his or her aggressive or sexual impulses have momentarily broken down, anxiety and guilt may be very appropriate reactions and may call for understanding of what caused those feelings rather than for trusting reassurance. Such a parent may be more relieved when the physician truly understands what has happened between the parent and the child and the reasons behind that disruption of a nurturing parent/child relationship than when the physician easily accepts an explanation that the parent knows to be untrue.

Secondly, in order for a primary caretaker to confront parents supportively, he must deal with his own feelings of doubt and anger. It can help if he understands that just as a somatic sign is merely a symptom of a medical problem, the abused child is also a symptom of a family in crisis. When only the child is perceived as the victim and the parents as negligent caretakers or as assailants, the physician normally experiences considerable anger. If this anger is not tempered with understanding of the parents' feelings and often multiple problems, fear, frustration, sense of isolation, depression and helplessness, it will be expressed in an accusatory manner devoid of the compassion which parents who may already feel beseiged need to accept the concern of the physician for the child's well being.

When the physician recognizes the positive aspect of abusive parents, he can seek to align himself with that portion of their personalities by recognizing and acknowledging their wish to protect their child from further injury and distress. He can use this groundwork for effectively dealing with abusive treatment. If the physician's communication to parents is expressed with concern and compassion for the entire family, the protective aspect of reporting can be emphasized and the parents may be relieved that their plight has been recognized rather than provoked into adopting a self defensive posture.

It is often useful for the physician who does not recognize that he is dealing with an abusive situation to seek social service, psychiatric and legal consultation. It's useful for him to be sufficiently familiar with reporting forms to be able to go over them in detail with the parents. The physician who can accurately describe to parents the immediate consequence of a report will be able to protect them from unreasonable and unwarranted fears, facilitate their willingness to be cooperative and reaffirm his role as a forthright and trustworthy friend of the family. He should be prepared to answer the parent's questions and to assure them of his willingness to seek answers not immediately possible to provide. He should be prepared to offer the family continued care by making it clear that he is not merely fulfilling his mandated duty but he is also initiating a process in which he will continue to be involved as an advocate for both their child and themselves.

The physician's fear of losing control of a case or of turning a family over to an unknown fate at the mercy of overwhelmed, impersonal, insensitive state agencies can be ameliorated considerably by his continued active involvement with both the family and the personnel of the agency empowered to investigate.

In addition to writing a report, the physician should contact the assigned worker in order to assure that both the worker and the family have continued interest. Most public agencies are overextended and grateful for whatever ongoing assistance the referring physician may be able to provide by actively consulting with workers who will be involved in subsequent phases of family assessment intervention.

Managing One's Anger

Once abuse has been suspected and duly reported, the physician must be wary of the anger which such situations engender. Having attempted to understand social, economic, and psychological stresses with which the parents have struggled and having sought to restrain his own propensity to feel enraged with those who would ignore or injure a child, it becomes necessary to recognize that this anger is still felt by virtually every professional dealing with such cases. Despite compassion and understanding, this anger will not go away. Expressing anger towards the family is notoriously counterproductive, however, as one struggles to muster all the resources possible to support the parents' efforts to gain control of themselves and their situation so that they can become more effective and protective caretakers.

Consequently, the anger often emerges in disguised forms. It is displaced or directed against others rather than against those who have inflicted the injuries directly. In virtually no other psychological situation is there more risk, more propensity to interdisciplinary/interagency conflict and criticism than in dealing with child abuse. Often, anger is manifested by exaggerated and unrealistic expectations about the responsiveness of protective service workers, social workers, psychologists and psychiatrists. When attempting to protect the vulnerable child, the kind of honest disagreement about diagnosis and appropriate courses of action which could constitute routine, interdisciplinary discussions in other situations become exaggerated, personal, intense and sometimes frankly hostile. While striving in what one earnestly believes to be the best interest of the child or a family, it is easy to believe that anyone who perceives the situation differently, who does not respond as thoroughly and as sensitively as one might hope, is as negligent and abusive as the family itself.

Rather than functioning as physicians, social workers, and psychologists, there's a great temptation to become either public defenders on the one hand or child savers on the other. In the former role, there's a tendency to defend the integrity of the family at all costs against the intrusion of social agencies, to take to task all agencies who do not provide the most comprehensive and salvatory services imaginable. In the latter role there is a tendency to overlook the assets and good intentions of parents who may have faulted in their responsibility under stress. There may be difficulty perceiving that the damage done by prematurely disrupting the continuity of care, rupturing essentially positive emotional bonds between a parent and a child, insulting the self esteem of both parents and children by precipitously removing a child from a situation which might seem potentially dangerous may outweigh the risks in attempting to bolster a difficult situation, however formidable that task may appear.

There's an enormous tendency to be aware that expressing anger towards the family is counterproductive but a failure to recognize that often that anger gets displaced upon the people we work with. When we find ourselves responding to colleagues in a doubting, angry way, we need to raise the question: Is this simply a way of managing those feelings that the cases stir up?

* * * * *

—I think that one of the realities that we as professionals have to learn to live with in child abuse cases is to accept the fact that we can't have the situation we would ideally prescribe. You know, children grow up in a multitude of kinds of situations and the situation that is realistically possible for this child may not be that which we consider best in our fantasy of the way we would like to have this child raised.

One of the frustrations of our position of seeing victims without victimizers is that as we become more enlightened we know that we can't blame the parents—that parents are victims as much as children. We can't blame social workers because social workers are victims as much as the parents. And the circle of responsibility becomes wider and wider, and I think as that happens we begin to feel more and more impotent in terms of making any difference and also in terms of placing our anger anywhere at all that seems correct or just.

What mechanism is it that is often set up in medicine to not permit the expression, admission, and sharing of those feelings? Very often there is a stake in the medical profession in seeming invulnerable to each other and to patients and seeming so inhuman that we can deal with anything, that we can deal with things without compassion or passion or feelings. We can't afford to show our vulnerability to each other and that seems kind of a crucial question that is raised, especially here.

It seems to me that there is a dynamic basis for what you were saying about the importance of getting protective help for the child. In my experience in a variety of different contexts, the greatest fear that violent people have is the fear of losing control of their violence. The more we can let people know that the internal controls on their violence which they're lacking can be and will be made up for by external controls when they are needed, the more I think we actually reduce the anxiety and the proneness to violence of people who are out of control or fear being out of control. This concept might alleviate the guilt of the physician in a position of calling on outside help to bring in some external controls for parents who, however much they might protest, will in the long run be much more reassured by the presence of an effective external control.

Do you ever feel that there are situations where an accusatory attitude is an appropriate form of dealing with the parent—not in the sense that the emotional tenor of your comments is angry, but that the message clearly stresses the irresponsibility of the parent or the parent's need to change or seek assistance in making changes?

HR: Absolutely, but I think the distinction between an angry attitude and confrontation with an opinion is not always an easy thing to tease apart. What is needed is recognition that the parents are, at least episodically, out of control and need to have that recognized by someone who's saying, "Look I'm not necessarily angry with you for being out of control, but I am concerned and I am going to bring all forces possible to bear to help you get in control because not only is the child endangered but you'll have trouble living with yourself if that danger is not controlled more effectively."

The question is at what point do you say, "We'll look at the parents as the victim and search for the responsible person beyond the parent," and at what point do you say, "Look, we're dealing with the parents, they're the immediate cause of the problem and they're the ones who we have available for treatment and it's going to take five years to get adequate funding. In the meantime we have to deal with the immediate cause and we have to treat them not as victims or not only as victims, but themselves as causal agents." I don't know the answer to that question. I figure it depends very much on the parents' capacity to change.

—I think that what you do when you make a decision to protect a child is to protect the parents. If we assume that parents are not hitting their child because they want to harm them but because there are conflicts and an enormous amount of stress, then by not assigning guilt per se but assigning responsibility both to ourselves and to the parents and appreciating where that responsibility can and cannot lie at this point, we can take measures to protect both children and parents without taking a moralistic tone of blaming as guilty or evil anybody within that immediate environment.

HR: I don't think instilling of guilt is the answer. I think that what guilt motivates in people is a wish to alleviate the guilt. The way they go about alleviating the guilt is often destructive. It seems that what we want to do is not get people trying to alleviate their guilt but rather free up their capacities for self control and for being able to care about the children that they have.

—I think you can make a distinction between giving someone responsibility for something and blaming. It's been my observation that when we talk about stress interviews and confrontations with a family, it is more likely to be a family that's white and middle class as opposed to poor and minority. There's almost a reluctance to confront poor families because of the fear of racism or the fear of social class bias.

BIBLIOGRAPHY

Rosenzweig HD: Some considerations of the management of child abuse: a psychiatric consultant's perspective, in Newberger EH (ed): *Child Abuse.* Boston Little, Brown, 1982.

Schmitt B, Kempe C: Neglect and abuse of children, in Vaughn V, McKay R (eds): *Nelson Textbook of Pediatrics,* ed 10. Philadelphia, WB Saunders, 1975.

Snyder JC, Bowles RT, Newberger EH: Improving research and practice on family violence: potential of a hospital-based training program. *Urban Soc Change Rev* 1962;15:3-7.

Steele BJ, Pollock CB: A psychiatric study of parents who abuse infants and small children, in Helfer RE, Kempe CH (eds): *The Battered Child.* Chicago, University of Chicago Press, 1974, pp 80-133.

CHAPTER 12

Police Discretion and Family Disturbances: Some Historical and Contemporary Reflections

Michael Feldberg

Throughout their histories, American police departments have been first responders to family disputes, disturbances and violence. As many as one-fifth of all calls to the police involve violent or potentially violent disturbances, of which family disturbances are a significant proportion. In response to the possibility of injury or death to the victims of family violence, several states have altered their laws relating to the police handling of family disturbance calls, and I expect that soon virtually all states will have made similar changes. The most salient feature of these new laws is that police officers are now *required* either to offer shelter to the victim of family violence (and her children, presuming the victim is a mother) or to arrest the victim's assailant. Prior to these new laws, police had the option of offering a ride to a friend or a relative's house or a shelter, and could only arrest the assailant on a specific complaint of the victim (which many victims are afraid to make), or if the officer actually saw the assailant strike the victim. Now, in the affected states, officers may make an arrest when they have reason to believe a felonious assault has occurred even if they do not witness it, and even if the victim does not request the arrest.

In effect, the new laws greatly restrict the discretion of police officers to resolve a family disturbance call without making an arrest or removing a party from the home. Many, if not most, experienced officers dislike this narrowing of their options. Police officers usually develop their own style of response to family beefs or family troubles which do not rely on arrest. Conventional wisdom in police circles teaches that arresting or otherwise removing a husband or father from his home should be a last resort only if other techniques for calming the combatants fail. Given what the police believe is the reluctance of spouses to press charges, of prosecutors to prosecute in family disturbances, and of social agencies to follow up aggressively on court referrals, they feel it better to resolve family disturbances informally, in the home, if at all possible. Historically, where there have been clear signs that a wife or child has been assaulted by a husband or father, the preference for handling family disturbances informally has persisted. Before we assess the effects that the new mandatory requirements for handling family disturbances are likely to have, allow me to review what I believe are the salient elements of police responses to family disturbances in cases where officers retain their discretion to improvise solutions. This review will include references to historical as well as contemporary police behavior.

In his remarkable examination of a northern California police department, the political scientist Muir identified four styles of response to family disturbance calls. My own classification scheme of responses is paraphrased from Muir's work. Neither he nor I have done enough research yet to know what percentage of officers fall into which response style nor which personality, organizational or other factors account for the adoption of a particular style by a particular officer. In reality, the circumstances of different domestic disturbance calls may compel an officer to vary his* style of response from case to case.

The Avoidance Response

Some officers simply hate to hear a domestic disturbance call come over the patrol car radio. Notwithstanding the evidence to the contrary — police folklore has it that more police officers are killed or injured in family trouble calls than any other type, and a young officer particularly may feel somewhat overwhelmed by the responsibility of having to solve the domestic difficulties of couples married as long as his parents. Other officers feel untrained to do the work of marriage counselors and family therapists. Some think that family disturbances happen only in minority and poor families, and that "those people" shouldn't be using the police to settle their personal squabbles. Finally, avoiders of family disturbance calls tend to define the calls as something other than real police work which they prefer to define as solving rapes, robberies, and other street crimes. They simply do not think that the police should be responding to fights among family members.

The typical avoider's response, when he cannot get another car to take the call, is to take his time getting to the scene hoping that the fight will be over by the time he gets there. Once he arrives, he attempts to terminate his involvement as quickly as possible. This might entail gaining entry to the home and threatening to arrest all the occupants if they do not quiet down immediately or making an immediate arrest on the basis

---

* The pronoun "his" will be used both for stylistic convenience and to reflect the reality of male predominance in police work.

of having witnessed an assault or asking whether the victim wishes the assailant arrested, receiving no for an answer, and immediately leaving on the grounds that without a complaint there is nothing he can do in the situation. As a consequence of this latter option, the officer leaves the victim in the vulnerable position he found her occupying, very likely creating the preconditions for a callback to the home which officers on the next shift will have to make. Research indicates that callbacks to family disturbances usually involve a higher probability of violence than do calls that are resolved on an officer's first visit.

While there are few records of the police response to family disturbances in the 19th century, a few officers have written memoirs of their most notable cases. New York police captain Jeremiah Petty recalled an incident in the late 1840s in which he became an avoider, although the reader may sympathize with his decision to adopt that style in this instance.

> One night I was on my post on Canal Street . . . I heard a woman shouting, 'Murder,' and I went to the house . . . There, in a cellar, was a woman half drunk; she said she had been beaten by her husband. He was a cripple, and was lying on some straw on the cellar floor. The walls were covered with the slime of lizards. I tried to get the man up, but he could not stand without crutches. I examined his feet and found they were frostbitten. The flesh had rotted off and the bones were sticking out. He was half drunk. It was a sickening sight. After cautioning the man to keep quiet, I left the place for fear I should faint, and the lizards would crawl over my body.

Petty probably believed, and rightly so for his times, that the courts neither could nor would impose any further suffering on the man in retribution for his wife's beating, and that the city's charity organizations had little to offer in the way of family counseling should the couple be brought to their attention. I would suggest that, with multiproblem families of the type Petty encountered, many police officers develop the attitude that it is hopeless trying to change their lives, and it is best simply to cut one's involvement as quickly as possible before their problems intrude into the officer's own professional life. In cases such as these, *mandatory reporting* laws may in fact be the best prod to make avoiding officers fulfill at least a minimum obligation to contribute to the solution of the family's woes.

The Punishment Response

This response also has a long pedigree among police officers responding to family disturbances. Captain Cornelius Willemse tells us that when he joined the New York Police Department in 1900, he walked a beat in an immigrant, working-class neighborhood on 25th Street, between 7th and 10th avenues. Willemse tells us,

> In a neighborhood like that, there are a great number of family quarrels and the policeman had to be the judge and the jury, the Appelate Division and the Court of Appeals all at the same time. I settled such quarrels in my own way, as other policemen were doing. Arresting a drunken wife beater wouldn't help the family. The wage-earner would be in jail, the children would be without food and the wife would come pleading to the court to discharge her husband so that the family wouldn't starve. No, there was a more effective method. Whenever a drunken man beat up his wife, I beat the man up myself and gave him a taste of his own medicine. Then I made him go to bed and stay there until he slept it off.

Willemse paints a typical scene of the times in which he "entered many a home to face a drunken man and his sobbing wife. 'What? Did you hit your wife? Oh, you did, huh?' Sock, and sock again, if necessary. So it went. I became friends with many of the Saturday night wife beaters after I pounded them as they deserved. And wife-beating grew speedily less along my beat."

In some officers the impetus to respond to family violence with counterviolence may stem from their particular psychological makeup, although departments attempt to screen out violence-prone candidates before they join the patrol force, retrain them if they get by the screening, or assign them to desk jobs if they are not reformable. Still, some violence-prone officers remain on the street, handling as many incidents as possible with the maximum use of force — particularly family disturbance calls. Such officers tend to justify their actions by saying that the courts won't do justice to wife or child beaters, so they are making certain that the perpetrator gets at least some punishment.

But it seems fair to allow that Captain Willemse was not simply a sadist when he handled wife beaters by "giving them a taste of their own medicine." Willemse was concerned that arrest was more of a hardship on the entire family than the violent measures he had to take to prevent further violence. I'm sure Willemse was sincere when he claimed that his methods cleaned up complaints of wife beating on his beat. One may wonder, however, whether the actual number of family violence cases declined, or whether the wife–victims were reluctant to summon police help if the responding officer was going to beat up their husbands.

The Negotiating Style

The third response to family disturbances, in which the responding officer undertakes to help the family resolve the issues that precipitated the encounter, is one that is closest to a clinical or therapeutic approach. It has been encouraged in some departments and a few have offered extensive training and set up special units to respond in a negotiating mode to family disturbance calls. Officers who employ this style in their regular patrol work may have attended special training classes on family crisis intervention or may have taken psychology courses in college. Others appear to have adopted this style spontaneously through a fit between their personality and their experiences in handling family calls.

The basis of the negotiator's style is to get the family members talking and to keep them talking until they have made some progress toward resolving their issues. The officer may spend time offering them advice on how to solve their problems or how to seek help in finding a solution and may even help the family make contact with a social agency. Such officers will take two hours or more on a family disturbance call, justifying this use of their time on the grounds that it obviates the need for a wasteful callback and greatly minimizes the possibility that someone will get hurt in the future. In short, the negotiator becomes a family therapist, one who uses the opportunity of a crisis to make a significant intervention in the family's problem-solving patterns.

But it is precisely this investment of time that the negotiator's style requires that raises problems for police administrators and fellow officers. Unlike most professionals, a police officer is a social resource theoretically on call at all times and available to all those who need his services — not simply those whose problems match his interest or skills. Particularly on Friday and Saturday nights, when alcohol contributes so much to an increase in the number of family disturbance and other calls, requests for an officer begin to back up on the dispatcher's computer, many of them seem to have a potential for violence and injury. In that context, an officer who takes himself out of service for two hours to handle one "domestic" is unfairly short-changing his other potential clients and is shifting the burden of his workload to other officers on his shift. Most departments have a rule of thumb that it should take about 20 minutes to settle a domestic call, and if it's not calmed by that time, then someone has to leave the house either under arrest or voluntarily. This allows the officer sufficient time to trouble shoot with the couple yet provides a time boundary so that the officers can get back into service. Many supervisors doubt the long-term effectiveness of officers spending extended periods of time trying to resolve issues that have built up over years of a relationship. They suspect that some negotiators in family disturbance calls are really avoiders of other aspects of the job.

In the late 1960s, psychologist Morton Bard and his colleagues at the City College of New York attempted to solve the problems of resources and inadequate clinical skills in patrol officers by obtaining funding from the National Institute of Justice to create a special family violence response unit in an upper Manhattan precinct. Bard selected a group of 10 officers and arranged their schedules so that at least two officers would be on duty at all times. Members of the unit were to take all family disturbance calls in the precinct whenever possible. The unit used a single patrol car which was outfitted with a file card system on each domestic call that had been answered in the precinct over the previous year so that officers in the unit would know whether they were making a first time or return call to a home. Bard and his colleagues trained the officers in family negotiation, crisis intervention, and psychology. He assigned psychology graduate students to supervise the officers in the handling of their cases and to provide counseling to reduce officer stress. He held weekly team meetings with the members of the unit in which they discussed common problems and their solutions. The number and outcome of the family calls in the experimental district was compared after a year to the number and outcome of calls in a matched control precinct in another part of the city.

Paradoxically, the number of reported family disturbance calls increased in the experimental precinct while it remained stable in the control precinct. This outcome may be accounted for by an increased willingness on the part of the citizenry to summon the family violence unit because it found the unit's responses more helpful than those of untrained officers. More puzzling, however, was the fact that the experimental precinct experienced an increase in the number of family related homocides during the experimental year, while the control precinct saw no increase. This fact could not be accounted for, except by attributing it to random statistical distribution. Perhaps the most clearly positive outcome of the experiment was the fact that during the experimental year, none of the officers on the unit lost a day's work due to injury at a family disturbance, while several officers in the control precinct lost days to family disturbance-related injuries. Perhaps the greatest value of a program such as Bard's is that it teaches officers to handle family disturbance calls in a diplomatic and emphatic manner, thereby preventing the officer from making himself the target of the family's anger. Perhaps, too, the support offered by Bard and his colleagues had a kind of Hawthorne effect, keeping the officers' morale up to the point where even if they suffered an injury in a disturbance they did not allow it to keep them from missing work.

The Professional Detached Response

This style tries to strike a balance between empathic involvement in a family's woes and controlling the officers's time and commitment to any single call. Muir describes one such professionally detached officer responding to a family disturbance, officer Joe Wilkes.

> Joe Wilkes . . . perceived each family member as the center of a complex of relationships. When those relationships pulled the members in conflicting directions, paralysis set in or frustration erupted. When

those relationships pulled in the same direction, they created a force too great for any policeman to counter . . . In short, Joe Wilkes realized that any chance for a long-run pacification of a family squabble depended on the family's reattaching themselves to those friendships, traditions, and concerns they had previously felt were important.

To reattach a family, Wilkes would scan a home for the symbols of a family's commitments and hopes, "to scent out the glue that had held their center." Wilkes would compliment the wife for having a clean kitchen or comment on a good-smelling stew cooking on the stove. He would pick up a wedding picture and tell the couple how nice they had looked together, or point to a child's toy and ask the parents to talk about their kids. He would latch onto "anything which indicated the locus of former concerns, which had been beloved, any basis for hopefulness," and he would try to get the couple or the family to talk about its dreams for the future.

Thus far, Wilkes's style does not sound very different from a negotiator in a similar set of circumstances. But Muir identifies the important difference between them.

> In the end, however, after diverting, calming, reminding them of the meaningfulness of their old attachments, Wilkes took a chance. He left. He did not explore their problems in any detail. He did not know whether his citizens would injure one another before their former attachments had time to reassert themselves . . . It was not the safest course, but it was a calculated one, based on experience and a willingness to take risks.

Muir also argues that it is the response best matched to a situation in which the officer is "incapable of erecting sufficient protections around family members," for "such fences had to be perfected by discord and autonomy" reserved to the family itself. The challenge of regaining hope led to the possibility of moral growth for the family, and the skill of solving family disputes in this manner led to Wilke's moral development as an officer. It also left him free to fulfill his compelling obligations to society, since he had "learned to compromise treatment in the name of time."

Summary

As a society, we are faced with choices in how we shape our police officers' responses to family disturbances. It takes time, talent, training and good leadership by example for an officer to develop the professionally detached style of a Joe Wilkes, and of course the style offers no guarantees against the escalation of conflict after the officer departs. In addition, I would argue the style might be adopted more frequently by a larger number of officers if they believed that other support and social service systems were available to serve families who resort to violence to resolve or continue their disputes. As long as so many officers distrust the courts they will continue to mete out punishment on their own, or treat all family disturbance calls as hopeless cases not worth the emotional and physical effort they demand. As long as negotiating officers believe themselves to be more effective and available than family counseling services, they will continue to overstep the role that their training and their mandate equips them to fulfill.

In closing, I would like to make a plea to the social service and therapeutic professions to become more actively involved in training and referral programs involving the police. Given the severe cutbacks in funding to most police departments, they do not have the internal resources to set up specialized family violence response units, and this may be all to the good, since *every* officer should be trained to handle such calls. But where will the training resources come from? Again, in these times of strapped municipal budgets, I think the resources will have to come from outside, and trainers come from the ranks of social service and mental health professionals. Equally important, social agencies need to establish much closer referral and follow-up links to officers who respond to family disturbance calls. It is not enough to train officers to respond to family calls when less than 5% of these families actually make contact with a family counselor. Successful models for police/social service referral systems exist and should be implemented in more jurisdictions as quickly as possible.

Finally, in the absence of voluntary efforts at collaboration between the police and the social service community, legislatures will no doubt continue to pass mandatory arrest and reporting laws, compelling the police to abdicate responsibility for deciding who can safely remain at home and who must be separated physically. And who is to say that this is a bad thing in and of itself? In the face of current mishandling of family violence cases by some police officers, perhaps it is the best we can do. But if Muir is correct, mandatory reductions in a police officer's discretion rob him of the opportunity to develop morally. He becomes a candidate for early burnout on the job, unable to respond creatively not only to family violence calls but to the great variety of calls in which citizens ask him to solve their problems and offer assistance. Perhaps the cost of safety in one area is an overall increase of risk in others as officers become mere technicians, administering the imperatives of inflexible law.

BIBLIOGRAPHY

Bard M: *Family Crisis Intervention: From Conception to Implementation.* Washington, DC, US Government Printing Office, 1973.
Breedlove RK et al: *Domestic Violence and the Police.* Washington, DC, Police

Foundation, 1977.

Hanewicz W, et al: Improving linkages between domestic violence referred agencies and the police. *J Criminal Justice* 1982;6:493-503.

Michaels RA, Treger H: Social work in police departments. *Social Work* 1973;18:67-75.

Muir WK Jr: *Police: Streetcorner Politicians*. Chicago, University of Chicago Press, 1977.

CHAPTER 13

Parents and Practitioners
as Developmental Theorists

Carolyn M. Newberger

Everyone is a theorist. The notion that people who make theory and who do research to test theories are somehow different from the rest of us is not true. We all construct theories and these theories enable us to deal with the complexities of experience. Our theories about what is important tell us what to look for, and theories of why things happen enable us to anticipate future events and guide action.

We have theories both in our lives at home and in our professional lives. We do not, however, always know what our theories are. All of us in clinical work operate out of our gut some of the time. When things go wrong, or when things go right, we do not always fully understand why. Often underlying what we perceive, how we interpret our experiences and our response to those experiences are implicit assumptions. When we make our assumptions explicit they can be examined, systematically communicated to others, and we can confront what we select and acknowledge what we exclude.

Theories have developmental paths, just as persons and relationships have developmental paths. As applied to theories, developmental paths move from a more restricted focus with a limited selection of information, to a broader range with a richer integration of information and points of view.

What about child abuse? What are the theories that undergird our work? In this field, our theories tend to be at the earlier end of this developmental path. Until recently, the field has been dominated by unitary theories which take into account only limited dimensions of experience and exclude other dimensions of potentially critical importance to family functioning. Some of these theories may be familiar.

Psychodynamic theory basically posits that the cause of child abuse is psychopathology within the parent. Environmental theory claims that the reasons parents beat their children reside in the environment and have to do with environmental stresses. Attachment theory suggests that a process of bonding between parent and child occurs during the neonatal period, and if thwarted, the parent-child relationship is highly vulnerable to violence. In social learning theory, the predominant belief is that violence in the family is a learned behavior: a replaying of violence in previous generations. As clinicians, however, we find that we cannot rely solely on one or another unitary theory. Our clients are too diverse in experience and personality, and their personal pictures too complex for any one unitary theory to provide sufficient richness of either causal explanations or intervention alternatives.

Thinking in the field is developing, and different theoretical points of view are increasingly being considered both in building more comprehensive theories and in understanding the complexity of individual cases. For example, when you see a parent in a child abuse situation, I am sure you take into account not only personality structure, but also the environmental stresses that a family is dealing with, their strengths, and the resources that they draw upon. You look at interactions. You look at environmental stresses in terms of their interaction with basic personality weaknesses because not everyone who is stressed is going to abuse a child.

The field of child abuse, in general, is shifting from an emphasis on finding a common explanation for every child's maltreatment, to a recognition of individual differences; and shifting from the need to find theoretical closure, to the possibility of building theory which enables us to elaborate and continue to generate our understanding rather than to foreclose understanding. Each theoretical approach which has been applied to child abuse illuminates a particular content area, and certainly not all content areas which may influence family violence have been elaborated. Although we have different theories, we have neither all the theories that we need, nor ways of integrating different theories so that a more developmentally comprehensive basis for research and practice is available. Let me suggest some areas that are particularly in need of further examination.

Child temperament is poorly understood in relation to child abuse. Children differ; some are harder to raise, some are easier. Some children's styles seem to fit well with their parent's temperament. Sometimes a parent will have a child with a temperament that is very different from his or her own and will find it difficult to understand, to respond to and to deal with the child.

Another important area for exploration is *community resources and supports*. How do community institutions strengthen and protect? This area is given short shrift in research objectives of funding institutions in this country, yet we need to look more at what strengthens families. To understand child abuse or family violence, we need to know what makes some people able to function well given what may be defined as predictive indices of risk.

A third poorly studied and understood area concerns *cultural differences*, not only in terms of other societies and parts of the world, but also in terms of cultural differences within our own society. We inadequately understand what it means to grow up in Appalachia, what it means to be a migrant farm worker, what it means to be an immigrant from the West Indies, and how this relates to child-rearing practices. Sometimes we overlook the fact that our society has more than a single culture.

The fourth understudied area is *parental theories* or belief systems about children and the parental role. The work of other investigators suggests that parental theories and beliefs may importantly underlie how parents understand and act with their children (Aldridge et al, 1974; Berg, 1976; Egeland and Brunnquell, 1979). This has been the focus of my own research and forms the basis of my presentation.

We have been talking so far about how we are all theorists and how theory has been constructed and applied to the study of child abuse. Parents are theorists too, and their theories about childrearing may also follow a developmental path. What I have tried to do in my research is to make explicit parent's theories about children and about the parental role. I call this parental awareness. If we can understand the process and pattern of parental awareness, perhaps we will have some better sense of which kinds of awareness may be related to strength or vulnerability in families.

Now what is parental awareness? It is defined at this point as an organized knowledge system. It embraces theories of right and wrong, cause and effect which the parent draws upon to make sense of the child's responses and behavior and to formulate policies to guide his or her own action. There appear to be two dimensions of parental awareness. One is a perspective-taking dimension: how the parent conceptualizes the child and the child's experience from the child's point of view. The second is a moral dimension: the parent's concept of rights and responsibilities of the parent in relation to the child.

Let me explain what I mean by the moral dimension. Lawrence Kohlberg (1969) has defined morality as the area of conflicting claims between people. The proposed resolution of these conflicting claims reveals the moral judgments on which action is taken: the person's concepts of individual rights, the concepts of responsibility to each other.

Now when a child enters a family, the child automatically brings conflicting claims. A person is trying to get a good night's sleep and his child is crying — these are conflicting claims. Throughout parenthood there are issues that have to be resolved between the child's rights and needs and desires, and the parents' rights and needs and desires. Sorting through these conflicting claims is what I consider the moral area of parenting. How does the parent understand them and how does the parent think it is appropriate to handle them?

Parents who abuse their children seem to think about their children in more egocentric ways. They seemed less able to take into account their children's perspectives, to see their children as separate from themselves and having needs independent of the parent's needs. We find frequent mention of this phenomenon in the clinical literature, yet there has been no systematic way of measuring or studying it. But some researchers have, for example, noted that parents who abuse their child seem not to be able to empathize with their children as readily as other parents do (Berg, 1976). Others have noted that many parents do not seem to be able to recognize the consequences of their acts for their children. These kinds of observations, both in the literature and in my own experience, suggest that the cognitive developmental approach to how people construct or understand human relationships might be a useful way to understand something about parental function.

In childhood, the cognitive development of social understanding has been found to proceed from egocentrism to a stereotypic notion of others, to an understanding of others as unique. The focus moves from understanding others exclusively in terms of one's own experience, to an awareness of the perspectives and the intentions of others. To apply this to parenthood, researchers sought individual differences in the parent's construction of the child and of the parental role. These differences were hypothesized to represent developmental stages of social cognition in parenthood. I call this construction *parental awareness*.

To study cognitive development in parenthood, a set of developmental levels was constructed *a priori*. If parental understanding of children follows a developmental path that roughly parallels the development of children's thinking from egocentrism to a stereotyped notion of people, to an understanding of others' perspectives, how would that work for parents? After defining levels in a preliminary way, an interview was constructed based around a set of issues or tasks of the parental role. Each issue examines a task of parental understanding to be solved. A set of interview questions was developed around each of the eight issues. Each question probes a parent's understanding of the child – the reasoning that a parent uses to justify beliefs about how each of these issues should be resolved. It is in the justification of their beliefs that the theories that underline parental choices are found.

Let me describe the issues. The first is identifying influences on the child's development and behavior. This involves identifying the elements in the child and in the environment that the parent believes affects the child's behavior and development. The second issue is understanding subjectivity. What are the child's thoughts? What are the child's feelings? The third is defining personality. How do we define the child? What are the qualities and characteristics which make up personality in the child? What are our values about them? What is a good child or an ideal child? The fourth issue is establishing and maintaining communication and trust. This has to do with defining what closeness is, what love is, what reciprocity and sharing are, and how they are established and maintained. The fifth issue is resolving conflict. What is conflictual for one parent might not be for another, so the issue is, first, identifying what conflict is and then, how to deal with it. The sixth issue is establishing and maintaining discipline and authority. The seventh issue is meeting needs, defining and addressing them. The eighth issue is learning and evaluating parenting. What makes a good parent?

By asking questions about these issues we seek to elicit from parents conceptions about the child and conceptions about parental action. In order to do this, I ask two kinds of questions: direct personal questions and hypothetical dilemmas. Here are some examples of the personal questions. What do you find hardest to put up with from your child? Why is that? How do you handle it? Why do you handle it that way? How does it seem to work out? What are your goals for your child? Again, I probe the reasons why, because it is these reasons that reveal how the parent understands the child as a person.

Hypothetical dilemmas were also used. One example is the working mother dilemma. This is an autobiographical dilemma which was very easy to construct. It tells the story of a mother and a 10-year-old daughter. The mother had been at home with her child. The child was now in third grade, doing well in school, and the mother was dissatisfied and didn't have enough to do. She wanted to find a part-time job and meet some of her needs to get out of the home, have other relationships, earn a little money and feel good about herself. She found a part-time job and she enjoyed it. But the daughter had to come home to a babysitter three afternoons a week. Even though the babysitter was very nice and responsible, the child wasn't satisfied. She asked, "Why do you have to go to work when other kids come home to their mothers?" The dilemma for the parent is to resolve the conflicting claims between the mother and her daughter.

The questions for this dilemma revolved around: What are the child's needs? What are the mother's needs? What are the child's rights to her mother? The mother's rights? The mother's responsibility to the child? The child's responsibility to the mother? How do you understand what the child is experiencing? Which is more important: that the mother work if that makes her happy, or that the mother stay home if that makes the child happy? Obviously there is no right answer to this, although we working mothers always think that we know what it is. There are many difficult issues that parents have to think about in the interview.

Fifty-one parents were interviewed from as broad a cross-section of parents as I could find. They came from the outpatient orthopedic clinic at this hospital and from the local suburbs. Thirty-five percent of the parents were black, 65% were white. There were mothers and fathers. They came from all social class levels and had different numbers and ages of children, fairly evenly distributed.

The interviews with the parents confirmed that the levels of understanding originally outlined seemed to be fairly descriptive of how parents thought about their children and the parental role. There followed a lengthy process of revision to reflect more precisely what people said on the interviews. In my research, parental conceptions fell into roughly four levels of understanding (Newberger, 1980).

Level one is the *egoistic orientation*. (Please forgive the name. Names are always inadequate.) At this level the parent understands the child as a projection of his or her own experiences, and the parental role is organized only around parental wants and needs.

The second level is called a *conventional orientation*. The child is understood in terms of externally derived definitions and explanations of children. These definitions and explanations come from tradition, from culture, from authority, from grandmothers, and from Dr. Spock. The parent understands the child not through looking at the child, but through other sources which the parent then applies to the child. At this level the parental role is organized around socially defined notions of correct practices and responsibility—what others think is right or wrong for a parent.

The third level is called the *subjective-individualistic orientation*. At this level the child is viewed as a unique individual who is understood through the parent-child relationship rather than by external definitions of children. The parental role is organized around identifying and meeting the needs of this child, rather than as the fulfillment of predetermined role obligations. At this level a parent can think not only of how the child is like other children but of how the child differs as well.

The fourth level is called an *analytic or systems orientation*. At this level, the parent understands the child as a complex and changing psychological self-system. The parent grows in the role as well as the child and recognizes that the relationship and the role are built not only on meeting the child's needs but also in finding ways of balancing one's own needs and the child's so that each can be responsibly met.

I would now like to give some examples of parental reasoning from interviews I have conducted.

In level one reasoning, parenting methods are chosen because they are successful in changing behavior which the parent finds undesirable. The criterion for success is suppression of the behavior, not changing the motives of the child. Keep in mind that one parent is not necessarily a better parent than the other; that is not the point of this. This analysis has to do with what the parent is able to understand of the child and the child's experience. At the higher levels the parent is able to understand more and has more tools for dealing with situations because the parent is able to take into account more aspects of the child and more aspects of experience that parent and child are embedded in. Now, let's go to the examples.

The first example is at the egoistic level.

Interviewer	What do you rely on most to get your children to mind you?
Parent	Threatening them with a spoon. I have one of those spoons with the little holes to strain peas and things, so I take that and I say, "If you are not good, I'm going to beat you with it." And they usually behave when they see it. I don't use it. But when they see it, they usually behave.
Interviewer	How does that seem to work?
Parent	They mind up to a certain point. And then they say, Mommy is not going to spank me, so I'll start all over again.
Interviewer	Why do you use that method?
Parent	It seems to be about the only method that works.
Interviewer	Do you think it's the best way?
Parent	Well, no, but I don't know of any other way that works as well.

The orientation here is toward a concrete method that will suppress the behavior that is undesirable. The concern or the focus isn't so much on what the child understands, but on what the child does.

* * * * *

—How do you understand that as being a projection of the parent's own experience?

CN: In this case it is because the parent was not able to consider the child's perspective in trying to figure out what to do about the behavior. This isn't necessarily a projection; not all of the responses are going to be a projection of the parents' experiences. They may demonstrate some other aspect that is characteristic of thinking at this level. There are many aspects that are characteristic of thinking at each level.

—The mother may not be making any effort to understand the child's perspective as to why the child is behaving a certain way, but she is making an effort to understand the child's motivation to change. She believes, I presume, that the child will see this as dangerous and will therefore change his behavior. The mother is saying that she is going to set up a motivation system that is designed to make the child think about something he hasn't been thinking about.

CN: That's true. But the limitation of the thinking is that it is simply a stimulus-response kind of notion. It is not really thinking about changing the child or the child's values; it is simply thinking about changing his behavior.

* * * * *

At the second level, the notion of defining right and wrong, of changing values, of seeing the child as being a repository of values who has to be guided in the right direction becomes the primary focus. Here we have an internal sense of the child, but only in a very superficial way.

At level two, the reason for discipline and authority is not just to change behavior but to instill standards and values. The parent explains why the child is doing something wrong in order to ensure the inclusion of the parent's standards into the child's developing value system. Here is an example.

Interviewer	What do you rely on most to get your children to do what you want them to, and not to do what you don't want them to?
Parent	We explain everything. We explain what is good and what is not good. And we tell them, we preface this is good, and go on to explain why. And they can make a decision as to whether they are going to go along with it or not. And then we will explain and try to reinforce our ideas.
Interviewer	Why is explaining important?
Parent	So they will know what is right and what is wrong.

At the third level the parent reasons that the cause of the behavior rather than its manifestation must be addressed. The why that the parent focuses on at level three is not just the parent's why, but also the child's why. At this level the parent appeals to the effect of the child's action on others, not just to the rightness and wrongness of an act. Let's get back to the subject of discipline for the example. (It is important to recognize that both parents in these two examples think of talking as the best way, but it is in the reasons why they think of talking that the differences emerge.)

Interviewer	What do you feel is the best way to get a child to mind you?
Parent	Talking.
Interviewer	Why is that the best way?
Parent	Because first of all, you ask questions, and you find out why they did it. And they tell you, "I broke it because you weren't paying any attention to me." So you find out, "What attention did you want me to pay? I was busy too. After I finish this, then we will sit down and we will have a long talk about anything that you want to talk about. Play any game that you want to." Meanwhile I'm finding out if it is just, "I felt like breaking it." "OK, I just felt like hitting you right now. So how about if I do that? No, why not?" "Because if you

hit me it will hurt." "You hurt me by breaking my vase." I'll handle it like that.

At level four, the child is conceptualized developmentally. Physical and emotional needs and capabilities must be addressed when they are developmentally relevant in order for other kinds of growth to take place. This is a systems orientation. The focus is not only on the directly underlying explanation or motivation as in level three, but also on issues of the larger developmental and relationship process in which the issues of discipline and authority are understood to be embedded. Discipline and authority are part of a continually developing relationship process between parent and child which has both deep and superficial levels. Here is an example of that.

Interviewer What do you do to get Steven to mind you?
Parent It depends on Steven. What he seems to be asking for at different times in his life. Right now he has been testing me a lot. He seems to be asking me for controls.
Interviewer What do you mean?
Parent Children can test you to see how much they can get. How much freedom they can get and to know their boundaries. Yet it is a pull both ways. Steven is trying to test me, plus he wants my comfort and attention and concern. I think if I do control him, he knows I am concerned. Deep down inside he knows that it is for his own good. He can still want something and know that it is dangerous, and be grateful at some level to a person for telling him that it is for his own good not to do that.

What this work is trying to do is find a structure for making explicit the theories or belief systems that parents construct about their children and about child rearing. The focus is not on what people do, but on their cognitive guidelines. One reason that it seemed that a developmental measure would be useful is that most of our theory on parents is not developmental. It does not deal with the path through which people progress from perhaps less adequate understanding to more adequate or comprehensive understanding. Research has not really dealt with the process of normal development in parenthood. When one looks at things developmentally rather than in terms of pathology, the same dimension can suggest what strengthens people as well as what renders people vulnerable. There is also a sense of where people come from and where people can go, which is important clinically.

How do we identify whether this is a developmental sequence? As you know, I studied 51 parents and saw them once. Obviously, what I can know is very limited, so let me explain how I addressed that problem.

As I said before, I am generating hypotheses, not testing them. In further research I will be able to formally test the hypotheses. Meanwhile, I studied development in three ways. One is through the logical construction of the levels.

Each level logically incorporates the preceding level into its own structures. When we think about children from perspectives other than our own, we don't lose our own perspective; it becomes a subset of how we view our child. Our view of the child then becomes more comprehensive and subsumes our own perspective; the egocentric perspective is subsumed in the larger societal perspective. The same is true with level three. We shouldn't throw away Dr Spock because we are tuned in to our own particular child. Dr Spock imparts important things about all children, and that is subsumed within our conception of our child as an individual who not only shares characteristics with other children, but also may be different in important ways. Then in the fourth level we can also step outside and see that there is a point of view that comes from looking at our own relationship process with the child. Each stage has to build from the preceding one.

But there is the empirical question: Can we see development in people's actual thinking? I looked at that in two ways. First I interviewed 16 children from the ages of 8 through 16 and looked at whether there is development in childhood of children's conceptions of the parental role and of children's conceptions of a child from the point of view of a parent. The interview questions were rephrased to read: If you were a parent, what would be your goals? If you were Mrs Smith, would you go to work? I found that there is a very orderly and strong unfolding of parental awareness levels with age. No children, however, got to the highest level. There were a few children who had some level three reasoning, but no children demonstrated level four reasoning. It appears that conceptions of children and the parental role do develop during childhood, but that for the development of the most mature levels, perhaps adult experience with children may be needed.

That raises the question of whether every parent begins at an egocentric level. People develop an understanding of other people throughout life and the parent-child relationship is but another interpersonal relationship. Probably what happens is that parents bring to the parent-child relationship their general understanding of other people. Issues particular to the parental role develop during parenthood.

To test the hypothesis that parental awareness develops during parenthood, a longitudinal study must be done following people from adulthood before they have children through their childrearing years and perhaps beyond. Obviously, I could not do that and that is one of the reasons why I say this is hypothesis generating research. I did get a sense of parental development, however, by looking at parents with differing years of experience. I compared parents with younger children with parents who had older children, and I found that when parents with the same number of children are compared with each other, there was a relationship between years of parental experience and parental understanding. The relationship is highly significant; that is, it is a relationship which would have unlikely occurred by chance.

Parents who had older children reasoned as a group at higher levels than parents who had younger children. Also, I found that when we looked at the relationship between how many children a parent had and their understanding, there was not a significant relationship. (There was a little direction upward if they had two children rather than one, but then if they had three or four children there was a bit of a direction downward. This was a pattern that could have occurred by chance.) But if we took all the parents who had two children and compared them, we found that the parents who had the older children reasoned at significantly higher levels than the parents who had younger children.

That is the issue of development. Another issue is what we call the issue of structure. If we ask if a measure has structure, we are asking if it represents stable patterns of thought that are applied consistently in different realms of experience. If I found that parents thought at one level about one issue and another level about another issue, or thought about the hypothetical dilemmas very differently than they thought about the personal questions, then I would say that the measure does not mean much because it does not represent a coherent aspect of a parent's theory system.

In order to see whether the measure did tap into a consistent belief system, I looked at responses from issue to issue and found that they were consistent. I also looked at the individual interviews and the patterns within the interviews to see whether parents tended to reason at one level or whether their reasoning was generally scattered. I found that a mean of 72% of responses were at one level. A mean of 24% were at another (and that was another adjacent level). So we found that parents tended to reason at one level but some of their thinking was either going a bit forward or was a bit behind. About 4% might be at a third level. For cognitive developmental research, this is a fairly consistent finding and is in line with criteria for a set of developmental levels which tap something coherent within the individual's thought system.

Another issue is universality. Are these measures descriptive of general parental thinking? Do they apply if people in the hospital are interviewed, but not people across the street? Again, as with the developmental question, this is a question that cannot really be answered without further research. All we can do is generate hypotheses from what we have. The best way, of course, is to do cross-cultural research and see whether there is a development of parental thinking which seems to correspond to the way in which development has been defined here. Since, at this point, this has not been done, what I looked at instead was whether there were differences in thinking depending on sex, race, or social class of the parent. I was also able to do an IQ measure with the children and see whether there were differences dependent on IQ. I did not find that the relationships differed significantly with any of these factors from what we might expect just by chance occurrence. Again, this is a small study and these considerations are very preliminary.

* * * * *

—In a Piagetian developmental view, you cannot teach a 4-year-old certain things, no matter how hard you try. You can get them eventually to say the right answer but they won't believe you and it won't carry over. I wonder whether you can teach people how to think about their children?

CN: The reason that you can't teach 4 year olds is that 4 year olds are not biologically ready. They have to develop adequate mental structures in order to be able to integrate that new information into their mental maps of how things operate. Whether a parent who reasons at an egocentric level does not have the needed cognitive structure, or whether other things are interfering remains to be seen.

* * * * *

Let me go on to parental awareness and parental behavior: obviously the critical question is whether there is a relationship between how parents construct their understanding of the child and the parental role, and how parents behave as parents with their children. Once again, this question should be answered with a different study. It should be answered by following parents over time and looking at the kinds of choices parents actually make with their children and their understanding of their own children.

I was able to address that question in a preliminary way by doing a study comparing eight parents who had abused their children with eight parents who had not. The parents were matched on race, social class, number and age of children. There were very strong differences between the two groups. In seven of the eight pairs, the child abusing parents had lower levels of awareness than the matched parent. When I pooled them together and looked at the difference between reasoning levels for the child abuse parents and reasoning levels for the matching parents, I found a highly significant difference between the two groups.

* * * * *

—One would expect a profound relationship because as the clinic and the social services system operate, parents are not going to end up in your abuse category or variable unless they exhibit a clinical lack of awareness.

CN: We do need to do a very different kind of research to sort out these issues. What I wanted to go on and say about the child abuse study is that not every parent who abused or neglected a child had very low levels of understanding. And not every parent with a very low level of understanding from the original sample had, as far as we know, abused or neglected a child. This brings us back to the notion that in the development of theory we have to look for elaboration, not closure. This isn't something that is going to tell us who is going to abuse or neglect their children; rather, it is a piece of information that helps us to understand what we may see intuitively. We have to look at what may protect families who have very low levels of understanding from abusing or neglecting their children and what may render some families vulnerable who appear to have higher levels of understanding. I looked at the cases and my data in order to see what those differences might be. I found that the parents who have very low levels of understanding but have not abused their children had much higher incomes than parents with very low understanding levels who had abused their children. (The criteria for matching people with social class did not include income in the calculation.) Secondly, the parents who had not abused their children were twice as likely to have a man at home—another adult in the household who, one imagines, could give a hand. Having a man in the household isn't always wonderful, but it may help some families cope who have limited conceptual resorts for understanding the child.

This table gives some sense of how I think parental awareness might interact with stresses (with the understanding that social environmental stresses are also only part of what we need to be able to know and understand).

Parental Awareness, Stress, and the Hypothetical Probability of Child Abuse

	Low Stress	High Stress
More Mature Parental Awareness	1. Least Probability of Child Abuse	2. Less Probability of Child Abuse
Average Maturity of Parental Awareness	3. Less Probability of Child Abuse	4. Less Probability of Child Abuse
Less Mature Parental Awareness	5. Less Probability of Child Abuse	6. Greatest Probability of Child Abuse

Cells 3 and 4 represent what we might consider an average level of parental awareness. We would have high parental awareness in cells 1 and 2; low parental awareness in cells 5 and 6. In cells 1, 3, and 5 we have low stress, and we have high stress in cells 2, 4 and 6.

The way it might work is that in cell 6 there would be a greater likelihood of dysfunction, and in cell 1 there would be the least likelihood of dysfunction. In cell 2, the likelihood of dysfunction would be lessened by the higher level of parental awareness. In other words, parental awareness may help to protect some families in the face of stress and enable them to raise their children with a greater degree of understanding and awareness than families who don't have those conceptual tools to use. Low awareness may render some families particularly vulnerable to abusing or neglecting their children in the face of stress.

Let me explain how one expands a theoretical explanatory model of child abuse. A clinician or researcher can look at the high dysfunction in cell 6 where it should be, and the high dysfunction in cell 1, where it should not be, and find out what is similar in those two types of families. Once the similarity is found a third factor is built in, and the theoretical model is expanded. The same thing with the low dysfunction. A third factor can be found, a supportive factor, which mitigates the expected effects of high stress coupled with low parental awareness—perhaps a strongly supportive extended family, or a compassionate social worker. Eventually there is a true three-dimensional model. Once that is done, the model can be split again and a 4th, 5th, 6th, and 7th dimension can be built. This is not done in current child abuse family model research, and if it is not going to be done, we will suffer with the same kind of myths and conventional wisdoms that exist now because of our limited understandings. If it is done, it will expand our knowledge base, and it will also profit the clinician who will have more than unidimensional theories to from which to draw.

BIBLIOGRAPHY

Aldridge M, Cautley P, Lichstein D: *Guidelines for Placement Workers.* Madison, University of Wisconsin Center for Social Service, 1974.

Berg P: Parental expectations and attitudes and child abusing families. *Dissertation Abstr Int* 1976;37:1889.

Egeland B, Brunnquell D: An at-risk approach to the study of child abuse: Some preliminary findings. *J Am Acad Child Psychiatry* 1979;18:219-235.

Kohlberg L: Stage and sequence: The cognitive-developmental approach to socialization, in Goslin D (ed): *Handbook of Socialization Theory and Research.* New York, Rand McNally, 1969.

Newberger CM: The cognitive structure of parenthood: Designing a descriptive measure, in Selman R, Yando R(eds): *New Directions for Child Development: Clinical Developmental Research.* San Francisco, Jossey Bass, 1980.

Newberger CM, Cook S: Parental awareness and child abuse: A cognitive develpmental analysis of urban and rural samples. *Am J Orthopsych* 1983:53:512-524.

CHAPTER 14

Cultural and Ethnic Issues:
The Black Family

Jessica H. Daniel

I would like to deal with three topics: one is the research on the black family in America, the second is the experience of majority clinician – minority client relationships (and institutional contacts), and third is the experience of minority membership on a hospital child abuse team.

BLACK FAMILIES: THREE PERSPECTIVES

Black Americans have a rather unique status because of the social, economic, political and psychological factors in a racially conscious society. Research, while presumably objective, has presented distinct ideological perspectives on black family functioning.

Black and white researchers have different perspectives on black family functioning in this country. Three perspectives are the *cultural equivalent* perspective, the *cultural deviant* perspective, and the *cultural variant* perspective.

The *cultural equivalent* position is that there is no clear cultural distinction between black and white families in this country. Researchers refer to black families as culturally white or as black puritans, ie, black families who take on the morals and manners of the whites. More recently, researchers have taken the position that there is merely a social class distinction between blacks and whites – no real cultural difference – and that if in fact blacks and whites made the same amount of money, they would be basically the same in our society. In the cultural equivalent perspective, blacks who are similar to whites are acceptable, but those who differ from whites are deviant.

The latter is related to the second perspective, the *cultural deviant* perspective. The researchers holding this perspective recognize that in America black families do differ from white families. They see these differences, however, as deviancy, meaning that the black families are pathological. White middle class values are used as the norms, and any differences between blacks and whites are seen as indications of dysfunctioning. It has been asserted that at the heart of the deterioration of the fabric of Negro society (in the days when this line of theory was popular, most writers used the word Negro) is the deterioration of the Negro family. This perspective portrays the black family as basically pathological; deviancy here means defective.

More recently, researchers have taken the perspective that black families can be seen as *cultural variants*. They acknowledge a black cultural style as different, but not necessarily pathological. Differences are recognized in the environments which result in differences both in family structure and ways of functioning. Most importantly, black family patterns can be seen as adaptive.

It is important to be cautious in listening to the cultural variant position. There is a danger of viewing all differences as healthy, when in fact some differences are pathological.

One has to put all of this in perspective for a fair treatment of black families. I am presenting these research approaches in a critical way because what we know about family functioning comes in large part from researchers. They have ground the cognitive lenses through which we look at black family functioning in America.

Healthy Functioning

The lifestyles of black families are very heterogeneous. They vary a lot in terms of kinship structure, geographic location, values, and social class status. There is no one family which can be presented as the model for all black families. In the process of reviewing the literature and looking at the more recent research on black families, particularly using the cultural variant perspective, researchers such as Andrew Billingsley have identified a number of predominant patterns for healthy functioning. It is important to identify health before looking for pathology in black family functioning.

At this point I would like to review some of the healthy patterns of black family functioning. The first one is *role flexibility*. Historically, black family members have found it necessary to display flexibility in family role definitions, responsibility and performance. Children commonly assist with care and socialization of younger siblings. Afro-American family functioning can be understood as a continuation of African family functioning. On the mother continent, ie, Africa, older children play that role. Children as well as wives may share with the husband, ie, father, the economic maintenance—they are expected to contribute financially to the household. Also, there is less stereotypic expectation of male/female relationships and roles in the family. Research on the black family has found that the black male, in spite of his macho imagery, is more likely to take out the garbage than the counterpart white male. He is also more likely to cook and clean house and to do it with some proficiency.

The role flexibility is due partly to historic necessity, but also to some current realities. The reality is that most black households where there are two parents available involve both parents working. As Billingsley points out, the black middle class is to a large degree a precarious middle class. It is dependent upon the two-family income and if one parent isn't working, the family may slip into a lower income bracket.

The second strength of black family functioning is the close-knit *kinship system.* Generally, families are well integrated into large kin-friend networks. In the South many blacks are in close proximity to kin, and therefore the extended family is largely kin in nature. However, Harriet McAdoo in her research of black middle class functioning has found that in the North, in the absence of proximity to actual kin, middle class families have duplicated extended family networks by establishing friend networks. The networks are invaluable ways of supplementing the material, emotional, and social resources available to family members.

The third aspect of healthy black family functioning is that blacks, as is true of most third world culture people in this country, are *bicultural.* They draw on both mainstream American and black cultural values. People who do well in our society are those who are flexible in shifting from mainstream to subculture.

The fourth strength in the functioning of black families is the existence of *parallel institutions.* The black community has formed many institutions which are found in the majority of communities, eg, businesses, fraternal orders, professional organizations such as the National Medical Association, National Association of Black Social Workers and the Association of Black Psychologists. Parallel institutions are formed primarily because too frequently the majority institutions do not have policies and practices which are in the best interests of black people, and because leadership roles are not accessible to blacks and third world people within the organizations. The oldest black organization in this country is the black church. The hour between 11 and 12 o'clock on Sundays is one of the most segregated hours in this country in that various segments of our society go their separate ways to worship. The black church serves as a social welfare organization functioning during recession and depression times. It is also a place where black people are acknowledged and honored for their accomplishments.

The fifth strength is a *race and personal identity and pride.* It is very important for healthy functioning in this country that one identify with one's racial group. For most black Americans their identity is pervasive. There is no escaping it — they are black. Racial pride in the sense of group membership frequently gives one a sense of purpose or greater security in self. If you know who you are, you are better able to function. It helps the individual better cope with the frustrations associated with racial discrimination and prejudice. The literature on black self-concept has assumed that black Americans have a lower sense of self, poor self-esteem. However, the research does not support that notion. One reviewer deemed it important to review the literature to ascertain reasons why blacks feel good about themselves, when logically they should feel very bad about themselves. Black adolescents who are functioning well accept the reality of discrimination in the society. They do not deny it. In addition to accepting discrimination, they identify healthy role models in the community. Black achievement is often seen as the great doctors, lawyers, scientists, businessmen, entertainers and athletes. Just as not all whites will achieve at that level, the same is true for blacks. But there are healthy models of functioning in the black community, and those are the individuals with whom the adolescents identify in terms of models of achievement.

The sixth strength is the *pooling of economic resources* both by the family and by institutions. As I mentioned earlier, within the nuclear household generally both parents are working and sometimes even children contribute to the household. Within the extended family one is expected to contribute not only emotional support but also goods – if a person has and if other people don't have, then that person is expected to share with them.

In the Depression, all people and particularly black Americans suffered under economic hardship. There is a famous church in Harlem – The Abyssinian Baptist Church. Adam Clayton Powell's father was the pastor of that church for a number of years. During the Depression, given the realities of the social welfare system, the senior Rev. Powell felt that the people in his church probably would not be treated as other people in New York City with regard to receiving goods and services. Black ministers frequently have a great deal of power, and they use it. He basically said to the congregation, "Those of you who are working are obliged to hire people who are not working. Those of you who are working are also obliged to bring clothes as well as canned goods to the church. And those of you who are not working will come and receive clothing and goods from this church." So they set up their own social welfare system so that, in fact, many members of their congregation did not have to rely on the public sector for services during that period. That is an example of pooling resources.

Seeking help　How black families in the Baltimore area sought help in times of stress was studied in the late 1970s. It was found that during those times, 10% of them sought help from ministers, 14% from psychiatrists, and 5% consulted the staff at community mental health centers. But the vast majority tended to prefer the *informal* system, seeking help from kin and friends. Blacks in our society still tend not to go through the formal network for help. They are just as likely to go to their minister as they are to their psychiatrist.

WHITE PROFESSIONALS AND BLACK FAMILIES

The second part of this presentation will focus on majority clinician–minority client relationships. Most clinicians are majority persons. In many child abuse and neglect cases, the clinician is a majority person and the client is a minority. It fits the stereotypic presentation of the majority–minority interaction in terms of power and position. Mutual respect and equity are difficult to achieve and maintain under these circumstances. The family members do not feel that child abuse and neglect are the dominant themes in their family functioning. Yet the interviews and data collection would all seem to focus on these, without needed emphasis on strengths and accomplishments.

The black family may be nuclear or extended. In working with the black family some consideration needs to be given to the extended family. The black extended family, as with all families, spans the continuum from very healthy to pathological, depending on a number of variables. While the extended family is seen as one of the strengths of black family functioning in America, a reality is that sometimes the extended family is more of a burden than it is a help to the families identified as being abusive. Sometimes part of the role of the clinician is to help the person evaluate those bonds with a pathological family and develop new relationship patterns. Some of the child abuse families are isolated from the healthy extended family. An intervention may be to help reestablish relationships which may be supportive.

Isolation and Child Abuse

Isolation presents in different ways. It could be that a family has been abandoned or ostrasized by the extended family because members do not fit with family norms. On the other hand, they could be a part of the family that is trying to get away from the pathology of the extended family. In any event, the isolated black family is in great need of help in terms of being reconnected with the black community, not necessarily with the extended family per se, but with components of the black community.

Behavior in Institutions

For many black Americans a case of child abuse and neglect is a time where they become involved with institutions, sometimes due to court intervention. Institutions in the black community have varying reputations, some positive, some negative. What happens when black people enter institutions? What are some of the ways families are helped or not helped? These questions loom larger in the minds of blacks than of whites. The sense of vulnerability for low income blacks may be heightened in these settings due to previous negative experiences with institutions, including educational systems.

At times when blacks enter white institutions they may decide to be on the offense rather than be on the defense. In other words, "I'll get them before they get me." An example is when a father came to the emergency room at Children's Hospital with a child who had an injury suspected to be an inflicted injury, ie, child abuse. He confronted the staff in the emergency room in a rather loud and dominating way, saying "If I were a white professor at a local institution, you would not ask me these questions, and you would not accuse me of child abuse and neglect." There was considerable reality in his accusation. Professional status is a substantial protection from the labeling of child abuse and neglect. But it is incumbent upon the staff to say, "Well, it's true that sometimes institutions are not fair, but we are dealing with your specific case now. We are not going to resolve all of the issues of discrimination in our society, but the reality is that your child came in with an injury and the injury is something that is very worrisome and we have to work on that."

What are the other ways in which people show some anxiety coming into institutions? One is that they bring the entire family in for support. Sometimes people in an agency are caught off guard by entourages; they don't want to deal with groups of people. They ask, "Now who takes care of this child?" And the reply is "We all do." And the agency asks, "Well, who provides primary care, who gives the most care?" The answer, "We all have to be interviewed." While sometimes that is true, the reality is that they come as a group for protection more than anything else.

Another situation that we have found in the past is that some minority parents have come to the hospital with alcohol on their breath. The reflexive response is that she or he is an alcoholic. A possible explanation is they may have used alcohol to mobilize themselves to come to the hospital. This does not necessarily mean that they are alcoholic.

Another behavior indicative of being upset is asking many questions. It is interesting how questioning by a black father or mother may be perceived. Sometimes the perception is that this is a caring parent who wants to be informed. Other times the parent may be seen and labeled as being belligerent and difficult. Parents who come to a medical area or who are interviewed by social workers are concerned about the data collection process. They wonder, "What are you going to do with the data that I am giving to you? Will it be used against me to take the children away?" Remembering the majority–minority relationship, it makes sense to feel the possible loss of power experienced by the client.

Another concern families have in dealing with institutions is the degree to which the institutions will be empathetic toward them in general and particularly in that setting. In a stressful environment with people in white coats walking around in offices and looking important and imposing, sometimes black parents have a hard time responding to questions and asking questions indicative of concern. At times they may repress information to present themselves in a much more positive fashion. They are afraid that they will be misinterpreted. Unfortunately, the possibility that the latter will occur is quite real. An example of a recent case involved a child who had been placed in a foster home. The child had experienced some difficulties in school; the foster brother had decided to discipline the child by spanking him. The physician reported that the child had considerable bruising. The social worker reported the following: The foster mother initially indicated that she was the one who had administered the spanking, but later on said it was, in fact, the foster brother. This was interpreted as an attempt to protect her son from possibly being involved with the authorities, understanding the vulnerability of a black male. The foster mother was greatly concerned that the child had boasted in school that he had received a spanking and seemed to be quite pleased about it. She remarked that in the past when she had spanked one of her five natural children they had never gone to school and boasted about being spanked. The child felt a part of the family when he was punished as the others had been.

Corporal Punishment

Most Americans spank their children regardless of race and socioeconomic status. Many black people were raised with corporal punishment and do not perceive their parents or caretakers as abusive, ie, they do not see this as child abuse but rather as a way to shape children into responsible citizens.

One possible misinterpretation in child-rearing styles is that some black parents are seen as very authoritarian, which can be very worrisome to professionals in that they perceive that behavior as being restrictive. Firm control is important because many black parents experience anxiety about how their children will survive in this society. Many of them constantly remind their children that they are black and what that means in terms of people's perceptions of them. They try to build in some controls so that the children are not placed in vulnerable positions, ie, behaviors subject to misinterpretations.

In response to the civil rights movement, some parents have been less restrictive in their parenting styles, especially in the black middle class. Low income parents may continue to see their children as being vulnerable and a representative of the race, ie, their behavior reflects on some 20 million blacks.

Evaluating Black Families in Clinical Environments

Once a parent has been suspected of child abuse and neglect or having a child somehow at risk, it appears that the person's rights to privacy are dismissed. The patient is expected to talk openly about his/her background and family. For some people that is very disarming and uncomfortable. They are not familiar with talking about feelings, owning up to feelings, or being heard.

Part of the pattern of black survival in this country has been that some people have not allowed children to talk about feelings or to talk about being hurt. To open that up opens up too many wounds. It also made the parents feel even less helpful and hopeful than they really were, ie, they felt unable to protect their children from racism and discrimination. When children or parents were experiencing discrimination there was a denial of it; families were incapable of talking about it, or dealing with it openly. So the statement, "It must be really frightening to have a child in the hospital" is an understatement about that experience and some parts of life. Efforts may be launched to shut out feelings, to deny, to laugh nervously, to make light of the situation, or to make jokes that are inappropriate. Much black humor is making light of very painful experiences. The nervous laughter and the denial are all part of coping mechanisms which are sometimes difficult to understand, but in fact these mechanisms help people to survive.

Child abuse is a highly charged topic. Persons who work in the area are sometimes upset and anguished about the injuries sustained by children. To introduce racial, cultural, and ethnic issues in an already emotionally laden topic area can constitute an overload.

MINORITIES ON CHILD ABUSE TEAMS

Finally and briefly, a third world or minority person on a child abuse team can increase sensitivity to issues. It is also important for the team to be aware of the discrimination experienced by the person in the institution and in the outside world and deal with that as a reality. A sign of whether a third world person is an integral part of the team is whether the team can accept the realities of the sometimes differential treatment received by third world people on teams. When people are insensitive to this as an issue, third world people are less likely to participate on teams or to have their participation compromised.

Families are seen in ways largely determined by the research data available. The intent is to inform so that work with families can move forward taking an embracive and respectful approach. While some differences among families really are pathological, some differences are adaptive. Second, in the evaluation and treatment of child abuse and neglect the majority clinician, minority client situations can be problematic. It is possible for a good working relationship to develop. It depends upon the clinicians: the greater responsibility is on the clinician to be respectful of the client's particular culture and racial background. And finally, it is important for teams and working organizations to be multicultural. Having multicultural, multiracial teams can be a strain for both majority and minority persons. It does increase the likelihood that the majority population will be more sensitive to the minority issues, policies and practices.

BIBLIOGRAPHY

Billingsley A: Family functioning in the low income black community. *Social Casework* 1969;50:568-572.

Cazenave N, Straus MA: Race, class, network embeddedness and family violence. *J Comparative Family Studies* 1979;X:281-300.

Daniel J, Hampton RL, Newberger EH: Child abuse and childhood accidents in black families: a controlled comparative study. *Am J Orthopsychiatry* 1983;53(4):645-653.

Hampton RL: Institutional decimation, marital exchange, and disruption in Black families. *Western J Black Studies* 1979;4:132-139.

McAdoo HP: Levels of stress and support in Black families in McCubbin H, Cauble AE, Patterson J (eds): *Family Stress, Coping and Social Support.* Springfield, Charles C Thomas, 1982.

Peters M, Massey G: Mundane extreme environmental stress in family stress theories: the case of black families in white America. *Marriage and Family Review* 1983;1-2:193-217.

CHAPTER 15

Natural Support Systems in the Puerto Rican Community

Melvin Delgado

THE IMPORTANCE OF CULTURE

I would like to take a look at natural support systems within the Puerto Rican community. I am focusing on the Puerto Rican community for two reasons. First, I am Puerto Rican. Second, most of my work in the past seven years or so has been with the Puerto Rican community.

I would also like to discuss holistic health and the concept of mind and body, which is in the vanguard nowadays in the health sector but has been around for centuries in many other cultures. Lastly, I want to focus on some recommendations in taking a look at why folk healing does and does not work.

Folk healing and natural support systems have a great deal to do with child abuse and neglect. My experience with family court has been with families who are brought in for child abuse and neglect because they are using folk or herbal medicine. When looking at the case carefully, it is obvious that the medicine they are receiving is not what they expect or want and that they prefer to use herbs; neglect is not the case at all.

In taking a look at the interface of two cultures, Puerto Rican culture and American culture, I am lumping American culture together and not doing justice to most sociologists and anthropologists. In essence, when two cultures come together there is tension at the point of interface. We tend to view one as a deficit culture. In the service delivery literature there is heavy emphasis on what is missing. And in the point of view of the court, a deficit model sets the tone for legal proceedings on child abuse and neglect.

All too often we can come up with normative standards of what constitutes child abuse and neglect, not taking into account cultural values and definitions. I have yet to come across a definition that looks at child abuse and neglect from a cultural point of view. Many times that happens the same way with therapy. We can always rationalize why a group of individuals or a person cannot benefit from what we have to offer. In the case records of persons who drop out of treatment the labels range from, "client is resistant to treatment," "unknown reason," "client is hostile," "client cannot benefit from treatment now," to "client is not motivated." I have yet to come across a case record that said, "What we have to offer is not what that person needs or wants."

Illness and health do not transpire in a vacuum. They transpire within a psychosocial, cultural context. Often we focus on the psychosocial, but the cultural falls by the wayside. We cannot look at child abuse and neglect out of the context of a cultural definition. I will share some examples with you.

Health settings, particularly emergency rooms, are in a propitious position to link people, particularly Puerto Ricans and other culturally and/or linguistically different people, with services. Unfortunately, if cases do not fit into the normative set we start looking at the possibility of child abuse and neglect. And what happens is that a system that has very little stigma attached to seeking services suddenly becomes a formidable system which requires thinking twice before going to get services.

Under no circumstances am I saying that within the Puerto Rican community we do not have child abuse and neglect; I am questioning our willingness to label child abuse and neglect readily. It may turn out that a 10- or 12-year-old is taking care of two or three younger siblings. The police come in and say that the parents have abandoned the children. The police reaction is a failure to take a look at the cultural definitions. Or the family may be giving herbal medicine to the child instead of the medicine that the hospital prescribed, and a child neglect case report is filed on the family.

There may be situations where the children run away from home, and it has to do with some cultural definitions of what constitutes a role in the family. I've seen this a great deal with Pentacostal families who have a very strict kind of upbringing. They put structure in their lives. This may be fine for the parents, but when a 13-year-old girl who likes to wear platform shoes, makeup and nylons but cannot because of her parents' restrictions, goes into a high school setting where everyone else is allowed to dress that way, she will stand out. The moral of the story is that the family that prays together does not necessarily stay together.

We have to look not only from a cultural context but also from a class context. I think most of the cases that deal with child abuse and neglect deal with the poor. It's a lot easier to find child abuse and neglect among the poor. I have many upper middle class friends who were abused as children. For example, people who happen to be very well off can send their child off to academies year in and year out and don't have to see that child because they can afford to pay for room and board. Is that a form of neglect?

What I want to focus on now are natural support systems from the point of view of a strength rather than a deficit.

My first exposure to folk healing occurred in my family. I had family members who were mediums. And everytime we went to visit them we were always given warnings. "Watch out for Aunt so and so." "Don't go into that room alone." As we grew up we picked up a certain message.

I came across the topic again in graduate school in my master's program. I went to a social work school that was psychoanalytically oriented, and my field placement was the upper west side of New York and the lower east side, welfare and family court. Needless to say, Freud did not go over very well there. There was a woman on the street who was a medium. She had a third grade education at most, and she was packing them in. Most of my clients were Puerto Rican and they would come to me for the missing welfare check, housing issues and any kind of systems issue, but somehow the emotional issues, what I was really being trained to deal with, were taken elsewhere.

The Puerto Rican specialist basically functions as a social worker, psychiatrist or psychologist (Rogler and Hollingshead, 1961). If we were to examine the structure of the cosmology and the premises and methodology of the rituals, we would realize that spiritualists are psychotherapists. The premises are different. Instead of saying that emotional problems or health problems are due to biological or experiential events which are primarily the two explanations that we use in this society, we would say that emotional problems and maybe health problems are due to metaphysical events and, in essence, spirits. If we take that basic premise and start examining the procedure of training, interviewing styles, and therapeutic styles it is apparent that there are some great parallels. It was then that I started to look at natural support systems.

PUERTO RICAN SUPPORT SYSTEMS

In the history of America, most ethnic communities had natural support systems and still do (Baker, 1977; Valle and Vega, 1980). We tend to play them down nowadays. There are basically four types within the Puerto Rican community (Delgado and Hum-Delgado, 1982). The first one is the family. The family still functions in many ways as a social security system. Our concept of the family goes beyond blood definition, and it takes on neighbors and friends.

The second support system consists of what we call healers or folk healers, and I don't want to give the impression that I am talking only about the poor. I have upper middle class doctor friends who believe in folk healing. The "santero" or saintist is really a cultural variation of the psychotherapist. The medium, or "spiritismo" has origins in 19th century France, and also functions as a psychotherapist. The "santigador" specializes with children a great deal, and is a cross between an internist and a chiropractor. Last is the herbalist, a cultural variation of a pharmacist.

The third natural support system is the religious system. Although 90% of us say we are Catholic, I would say that only approximately 10% to 15% practice. If someone tells me they are Pentacostal, Seventh Day Adventist, or Jehovah's Witness, that's a whole different story. Basically there are systems of belief that go beyond Sunday — ceremonies three or four times a week, recreational activities — the closest parallel in this society is a crisis center. The Pentacostal Church functions that way.

If an individual is coming from a rural part of Puerto Rico or from a different part of the country and is transplanted to the United States in winter, which is much harder than summer, in essence this is an uprootment which leaves behind traditional frames of reference, boundaries, grocery stores and similar resources, and transplants him into a city that is very cold, both literally and figuratively, and very alien. The Pentacostal Church provides a boundary, direction, and a family. People who belong to the Pentacostal Church refer to each other as brother and sister. The congregations are small. If a person cannot get to the Pentacostal ceremony they will send a van for him. If they are sick, church members will visit. They will find housing, work, and counseling for other members.

But there are dilemmas in that when they talk about salvation it's the whole family that has to be saved. This is fine for the parent, but for teenagers who don't want to be saved and are forced to be saved there is a very strict upbringing. The Seventh Day Adventists are even stricter: no meat, no music, no dancing. I think that individuals who are undergoing a period of crisis and need to tie in with traditional boundaries, can tie in, engage and disengage. When the crisis is over, some leave.

The fourth type of support system is what I call merchant and social clubs. One example is a botanical shop which is a cultural variation of a pharmacy. Available are herbs, healing paraphernalia, statues, tickets to local dances, novels, incense, records and the like. They are by far the most popular place. What I call the orthodox commercial model still maintains some commercial functions. It carries the more difficult to obtain herbs and healing paraphernalia and may also employ the services of a healer. In essence, counsel is available at the same time one is seeking herbs. What I call an orthodox model, and the only ones I know of are in New York City, basically functions as a distribution point for other botanical shops. They deal with nothing commercial — no records or coupons or anything like that. They deal with herbs and healing. At the back of the room there is counsel from a healer; at the front of the room there are herbs for sale. These are the botanical shops. We also have grocery stores; some of us may not think of grocery stores as support systems, but they are. Food may be more expensive at a grocery store, *una bodega*, compared with Stop and Shop or Safeway, but one gets personalized attention, credit, food that no one else carries, healing paraphernalia, if there are no botanical shops in the area, information concerning community activities, local gossip, and referrals.

The social clubs have a parallel in the Irish and Italian social clubs of the turn of the century. Social clubs are ties into home towns in Puerto Rico. They go beyond a pool table, juke box and dominoes to function as a way of linking people up in a community when they arrive, for jobs, housing, health, etc.

Finally there is the "marketa" or marketplace. The only one I know of is in New York City in Spanish Harlem, and everything under the sun is available there—native foods, clothes, and other necessities. People go there for the entire afternoon and never go alone. It is a way for them to sort of rejuvenate themselves in many ways.

In essence, these are the support systems. I'm not saying that each and every one of them has access to all types. They are just a framework that can't be ignored when doing an assessment and looking at ego strengths (Delgado, 1982, 1983).

In focusing attention on the holistic aspects of health, I think by far the most difficult dilemma is posed by dealing with someone who has a holistic view of life. Our training throughout graduate school or any kind of education is not meant to deal with holistic viewpoints. We have separated mind from body.

It is a fact that most people in this world have a holistic view. People who have a holistic view do not necessarily fit into our structure of services. We tend to somatize; most of the symptoms that we present are couched in somatic terms. Invariably, you will come across "nerves." Nerves are by far the most common symptom that we have in our community. Now you may want to say psychosomatic, and if you say psychosomatic and they go into the medical wing then a referral is made to the mental health wing. Chances are they will never make it there because they are not crazy.

When there is a difference in expectations on the part of the therapist and the client or patient, then there is a difficulty in a therapeutic relationship. What will happen in a situation like that is that the client's expectations will not be met. We did one study in Worcester and we found that before people were satisfied with the services, they went to three different hospitals. And very rarely were the expectations dealt with. The same thing happens with mental health. I used to like to ask, "What is it that you want from me?" I wanted to see how realistic the expectations were, and if they were not. I would state why they were not being realistic. I would try and deal with it rather than having the person leave and say, "Yes, yes, I'll do that" and never come back again.

Intervention by Medium

Two case studies sum up many of the issues. These cases were based at Bronx Lebanon Hospital and are referrals from the medical wing to the mental health sector. The cases are true. Note how the mental health wing approaches the issue and then how the medium approached the same issue, and what the consequences were.

Case 1: Juanita Casas* is a 39-year-old woman, divorced for nine years, and living in this country for a year and a half prior to her first clinic visit. She was referred to the medical service following hospitalization for a kidney infection, and complained of negativism and anorexia. She was disoriented and talked circumstantially. She had many somatic complaints. Among them were loss of weight, complaints of having a lump in her stomach, stomach and back pains and sleeping too much. Speech was scattered and at times incoherent; auditory hallucinations were present. The diagnosis was schizophrenia. Although Stelazine was prescribed for Mrs Casas, she refused to take medication. Her explanation of her illness was that she had been all right until shortly before leaving Puerto Rico. A close friend there began to suspect that Juanita was having an affair with her husband and because of the jealousy had put a hex on her. This explanation was given to her by a medium in the Bronx whom she had consulted. The medium also gave her certain prescriptions, advising her to drink mint with cinnamon for stomach pains and to boil herbs in water and then soak in the water. According to the patient's reports during a clinic visit, both of these prescriptions worked. When last seen she claimed to be free of both stomach pains and backaches. To keep the bad spirits from bothering her further, she placed a small glass of camphor under her bed each night.

Case 2: Jean Montero is a 31-year-old woman separated from her husband and living with her five children. Presenting problems were nervousness, insomnia, feelings of depression, hearing voices and seeing shadows. She expressed feelings of worthlessness. She was bothered by pains in the head and felt dizzy. Her chief worry was not this. Her chief worry was an 8-year-old daughter who had a spell the previous year and had stopped walking and talking. Her acute depression began at the time that her husband abandoned her and the children. The diagnosis was a psychotic depressive reaction. Stelazine and Elavil were prescribed.

During the course of her clinic visits Mrs Montero revealed that some of the strong spirits were against her and had all her roads crossed. Her troubles began after her neighbors put a hex on her. They put powder on her door and thus began the fights between her and her husband, causing him to leave. Again she lost out on a housing project at the last minute, and her daughter became ill after the hex. The daughter was seen at

---

* These cases were taken from an unpublished manuscript by B. Purdy, R. Pellman, S. Flores, and H. Bluestone, titled "Mellaril or Medium, Stelazine or Seance? A Study of Spiritism as It Affects Communication, Diagnosis and Treatment of Puerto Rican People." Department of Psychiatry, Bronx-Lebanon Hospital Center, New York, New York, Undated.

various hospitals and her mother claimed that the doctors could find no cause of the illness. After a series of missed appointments, Mrs Montero reappeared at the clinic to explain why she had not come in to say that she did not need mental health services any longer. She was consulting with a medium who was really helping her and told her that she did not need the clinic's assistance. This medium, using a photograph of her daughter, was giving her daughter "dispojos" or blessings. Following a series of these treatments the daughter began crying for the first time and seemed to recognize the mother when she visited. Mrs Montero also began to feel her old mind clear and her "roads were becoming uncrossed." She had a letter from the clinic recommending her for a housing project left by the medium and was just informed that she would soon have an apartment. She felt that our pills had helped her to sleep but that the medium was uncrossing her roads.

We are talking about two different ways of viewing the same phenomenon. In essence, it is a different way of viewing life. I'm not saying that it is better or worse; I think that it is different. We may want to say that differences are fine. Unfortunately, it never stays there. For example, in the case just presented a worker from the family court took the mother into court saying anyone who believes in mediums and spirits cannot be an adequate parent. The worker honestly felt that way; it wasn't a question of being racist or oppressive or the like. The fear was that the spirits would start telling the person to kill the children.

Somehow we have thought that our mental health concepts can be applied to anyone under the sun—that if we have a Freudian orientation, it would apply to everyone. That's not necessarily the case. People who are different, the Haitian community for example, will require a slightly different interpretation. Our concepts of folk healing, just like our concepts of differences, have been conditioned. If I mention voodoo most people will conjure up in their minds people walking around like zombies. All we have to do is take a look at a 1930s movie. If I mention medicine men, most people will think of witchdoctors. We have been conditioned to think that anyone who has a different interpretation and different credentialing process cannot be scientific.

BIBLIOGRAPHY

Baker F: The interface between professional and natural support systems. *Clin Soc Work J* 1977;5:139-148.

Delgado M: Hispanic elderly and natural support systems: A special focus on Puerto Ricans. *J Geriat Psychiatry* 1982;15:239-251.

Delgado M: Hispanic natural support systems: Implications for mental health services. *J Psychosoc Nurs Ment Health Serv* 1983;21:19-24.

Delgado M, Humm-Delgado D: Natural support systems: Source of strength in hispanic communities. *Social Work* 1982;27:83-89.

Rogler LH, Hollingshead R: The Puerto Rican spiritualist as a psychiatrist. *Am J Sociology* 1961;67:17-21.

CHAPTER 16

Ageism in American Society

Jack Levin

Blaming the Victim

I will begin by confessing that I am not a gerontologist. I became interested in the situation of the elderly because of my work in the sociology and psychology of prejudice and discrimination against ethnic, racial and religious minorities. A couple of years ago when I had an opportunity to examine the literature of gerontology, I discovered many similarities between the experiences of some minorities and the experiences of the elderly. As I went into it further, I saw that the concept of minority groups seems to fit the elderly pretty well. When I say minority I am not really talking about numbers but about a subordinate position in a society with respect to power, prestige, and wealth; majority group, of course, is a group that has the power and the prestige.

One concept in the literature on minority groups is that of *blaming the victim* — the basis of problems experienced by minority group members is seen as being in their environment or their heredity. An example is the idea of the *culture of poverty* where the problems and the inequality between poor and rich people are explained on the basis of some presumed defect in the family or environment of the poor. The focus is on what is wrong in the minority group situation rather than on institutional problems in the wider society, such as discrimination and exploitation. I found similar *blaming of the victim* in the literature on gerontology.

The central concept in gerontology, the central idea in research for many decades, is an emphasis on decline, or deterioration — psychological, biological, sociological, economic and political deterioration — with advancing age. And this decline has very often been used to explain the problems that are experienced by elderly people in our society — problems such as their relative poverty, disengagement, segregation. In 1963 there was a very popular theory called disengagement theory that legitimized this perspective and set the tone for gerontological thinking for at least a decade; there are still journal articles based on this idea. I am going to do it a disservice by oversimplifying it. The basic idea is that it would be better for both society and the elderly if the elderly would just go off by themselves and prepare for death.

Even programs for the elderly have blamed the victim. Many of them are designed to fix something, make it better. The elderly don't understand about insurance. Their IQs are declining. They are pretty stupid. Let's figure out a way to raise their IQ. Let's not take care of any institutional problems in society. Let's focus our attention on the victim.

I am not so naive as to think that many human characteristics do not decline with age. There is no question about that, but many researchers have found a great deal of stability over the life cycle and, as a matter of fact, there can be quite a bit of improvement. For decades, research showed that IQ declines with advancing age. All of these studies were cross-sectional. They compared young people with old people and they found out that young people were smarter. They failed to control for different generational experiences or level of education. In the last 10 years, studies using longitudinal testing of the same group of people over a period of time found something quite different; some subscales of IQ actually increase through the seventh decade of life. People actually get smarter, in some respects, over the life cycle. The overall, overriding assumption, however, has been that of decline.

Even where decline does occur, it is a gradual process. It does not begin abruptly at age 65 or 70. It starts long before that and continues gradually over the course of the life cycle. As a matter of fact there is no such thing as old age except sociologically. Old age differs from one society to another. There are some places where it starts at 40, others where it starts at 70, some 55. In every known society there is a group of people called *old*. In most societies when people get old, they are promoted to a position of privilege and leadership. In our society old people are meant to disengage—retire, we call it.

There is no such thing as old age except by social definition because the aging process is itself a gradual one with no automatic cut-off point. How do you know when you are old in our society? It's very simple. In our society you are old when you are pushed into retirement. There are legal as well as social sanctions; for example you collect social security and you have to show your senior ID card in order to get a 10% senior citizen discount. Many old people will pay 10% more rather than say that they are old.

Everybody talks about the cheaters on welfare, but the opposite happens with the elderly. Many people over 65 have tremendous pride and do not want to show their senior citizen status anywhere. Would you like to tell somebody that you are old? It is the most painful status in our society. Except in a negative sense, there is little consciousness about age discrimination in our society. How else would Johnny Carson get away with his nasty jokes about elderly people? He couldn't get away with such jokes about other groups. There have been several studies of jokes and humorous quotations. The vast majority of them are negative when they make reference to old people. We don't distinguish between old, ugly and ill. If somebody is old and feels well, they feel young. If they are attractive looking by conventional standards, then they look young.

Prejudice Against the Elderly

I believe that the elderly are a minority group against whom prejudice and discrimination have been directed. Elderly people have group consciousness — a negative group consciousness that came about because of suffering. It is the same with blacks. Blacks came to this country on different boats from different places and many of them lost their cultural identity. They tried to keep it but it was almost impossible. Almost every minority group has a negative self-consciousness; the positive self-consciousness of blacks is relatively recent. Women got that kind of positive self-consciousness in the 1960s, but elderly people do not have it yet. I think that they will get it in the next 10 years, and there are some groups such as the Gray Panthers that try to instill it now.

I believe that the prejudice against the elderly is a cultural prejudice. By that I mean several things. First, this prejudice against the elderly is learned by the age of 4 or 5. Most kids by the age of 5 have very negative attitudes toward elderly people. They get them from parents, from television, and from friends.

Minority groups are infantilized; they are made to appear childlike. Old age is seen as a period of second childhood. The women's movement has said they don't want to be called girls. And *boy* was used with reference to blacks. Women, elders, and blacks are all made to appear childlike. It is not a coincidence.

In old age we cannot do anything right. What are we supposed to do? We are supposed to sit in our rocking chair and prepare for death. We are supposed to disengage. We're supposed to get out of the way.

As a cultural prejudice, ageism varies from one culture to another. Even in our society, for example, in colonial America elderly people were revered, admired, envied. There was some hatred because the elderly could have the power in Colonial America. This may sound incredible, but during the Colonial period many people would actually wear wigs and powder their hair in order to make themselves look five years older. When a census taker came around there was a problem in misreporting age because the average citizen would say that he or she was five years older.

As societies become more modern they tend to become ageist, and the status of elderly people tends to decline, but this is not necessarily the case. For example, some studies show that in Japan, despite the intense level of industrialization, elderly people are treated pretty well. The 61st birthday is something like the 21st birthday here. There is an Elder's Day and there are instilled signs of deference. In the Soviet Union, elderly people are given an adequate pension so that they are often adopted by their friends. They are taken into the household because they are not a liability, they are an economic resource and a source of strength.

Reactions of the Elderly

What happens as a result of cultural prejudice is that elderly people start to play a minority role. They begin to play the role of inferior in their relationships with the majority. Just as traditionally there was the role of the Negro or the role of women, now there is the role of the senior citizen. Some of these childlike stereotypes come into effect. There are three things that elderly people can do: they can accept this stereotype and accept their role, they can avoid it, or they can aggressively try to eliminate it.

Many old people try to avoid the role to which they have been assigned. Alcoholism and drug abuse can often be a strategy of avoidance. Suicide, of course, is the ultimate form of avoidance. There are also positive ways that people can avoid. For example, they can re-engage, or they can try to. They can remarry, for example, for which they are often negatively sanctioned by the family. They can try to get another job, but it is not easy when they live 100 miles from the nearest urban center. Some elderly people, however, have gotten jobs and successfully re-engaged. There is a very negative form of avoidance, and that is called senility. I do not know much about the physiology of senile dementia or organic brain dysfunction, but I do know that some investigators talk about senility as avoidance psychosis.

There are some people who do not want to overturn the role; they are gaining because they accept it. We reward people for playing the role. We call it social security for example. We say, "Now we give you this money. It's because you were a good person and you are going to play the role the way that you are supposed to. We will put you on the fun bus. We will supply you with a small income so that you don't starve. We'll give you these food stamps and the 10% discount out at Drug Fair." The problem is that these rewards do not attack the basic reason for the problem.

Causes of Ageism

Why does ageism exist? Why do elders in our society have such a low status? Why have they become victims? There are many reasons. First, young people fear competition for jobs; this fear is especially intense under industrialization and that is when ageism bloomed. Second, death is now statistically associated with old age. At one time in history a person was just as likely to die at age 16 as at age 66. But that is not true anymore, and many people would prefer to ignore their own mortality. We put on blinders and institutionalize the problems that we do not want to see. Another reason for ageism is that the nuclear family has not helped much. The nuclear family puts elders out both physically and in terms of playing any meaningful role. And finally, there are the pressures to retire when people do not want to retire. I think that is the most important factor of all, because status in our society is determined in large part by what we do for a living. Retirement by age alone, rather than because of some disability or need, has created a group of stigmatized people. What we have to do is end discrimination against older workers, compulsory retirement laws, programs designed to get older workers used to retirement with gradual retirement training, and penalties associated with employment under social security.

If we ask people who have recently retired, who have made an almost irreversible commitment to disengage, they will say that they like it. But I think that we have to look at some independent data. People who retire and cannot find meaningful substitute activities suffer from a higher rate of suicide, drug addiction, alcoholism, and there is much evidence that they are more likely to become senile. It seems that this data is more compelling than the data that we get from asking a person for a verbal response.

There are grounds for optimism that the status of the elderly may rise again during the next couple of decades. Do not be surprised if the words *old* and *elderly* actually lose their negative connotations. Even if it is only in rhetoric, the turnaround that has happened as a result of the civil rights movement ("Black is beautiful") is incredible. Clearly, the experiences of minority groups such as blacks and women may be useful for predicting the course of consciousness-raising among the aged. It seems that raising the consciousness of elderly people is the most important thing to do.

Just as clearly, the uniqueness of the elderly as a minority group has to be considered as well as their similarity to other minorities. Whites do not become blacks. Men rarely become women, except in some operations. By contrast, the aged draw their entire population from the young who have been socialized as majority group members to accept negative stereotypes and feelings about old age. As a result, age consciousness raising may be particularly difficult to achieve or, on the other hand, consciousness raising may be facilitated by a recognition of the inevitability of everyone's aging—a recognition that the young, too, may ultimately benefit from positive changes in the status of the aged.

* * * * *

—By the year 2000, one-fifth of the population will be elderly. It was around one-twelfth in the 1950s. And I was wondering what your idea is of the effect of that?

JL: About 16% of the population is supposed to be over 65 by the year 2000. Now it's about 12%. It is really not as dramatic an increase as it sounds, but it could mean more clout for elderly people. It is also very difficult to organize older people. The first thing that they have to do is admit that they are old, and they will not do it. Sometimes in senior citizen clubs, for example, there is actually a penalty for referring to any old business. They call it leftover business, because they do not want to talk about old. Old is a negative. And actually the elderly people who do the best are the ones who refuse to disengage, or the ones who don't regard themselves as old.

But it seems that we will raise the age of being elderly, the age at which elderly status begins from 65 to 70, so we may have a real problem in terms of political influence. In a sociological sense, there may actually be fewer people around whom we call old.

I think the difference is going to have to come with greater consciousness that the problems that old people experience are a result of the way that they are treated, not as a result of their decline.

—I have a question regarding planning for senior citizen buildings. We visited a senior citizen who is in his 70s. We found him depressed over a number of visits. He was active in many organizations, and he had maintained his lifestyle except that he was living in this building. He said it was depressing because every day an ambulance came to the building, and once a week someone died. I asked if he knew all the people who died, and he replied that he knew most of them because, of course, he is very active in the building. I asked if he went to all the wakes and the funerals, and he said that after the first year he decided that he couldn't take it anymore. I don't think that people who planned these buildings had any idea about the impact of having an ambulance come at least once a day and having someone die at least once a week. That is a lot of death and illness for a person to tolerate, particularly an active person. I could understand his depression.

JL: I could not agree more, and I don't have an answer. I have learned very little to help me in my own aging. Even among privileged elders who can afford to go down to Florida or Arizona and move into a "fun city", 25% never leave their houses. They do not go out once a day to get the milk—they do not leave. Yet people take surveys and they find out that elderly people prefer segregated housing. Well, of course they do. Wouldn't you prefer it if you were being victimized by young people all the time? You have to ask what the alternatives are.

I think that housing segregated by age is terrible because of the death and the illness, and because it isolates old people from young people. But very often the alternative is increased victimization, more isolation, and greater fear.

—Much of what has been said today has been on the degenerating disengaged elderly. Are you aware of any evidence or research that focuses on character traits or lifestyles of active elderly? Are ethnic background, education, and role modeling factors?

JL: If I had to give one factor, it seems to be the way people were when they were young. There is remarkable constancy over the life cycle. People who are depressed a great deal when they are 30 tend to be depressed when they are 65. And people who were active when they were in their youth tend to be active later on.

A really sad thing is that there are many authoritarian societies in which elderly people have the upper hand. And there is age-grading there, too, but in the other direction. Elderly people are the leaders and they are the bosses and they are the supervisors, and is that any better? Wouldn't it be great if age were less relevant to our interactions and behaviors? It can't be totally irrelevant, but couldn't we reduce the relevance? I don't want to see the opposite happen either. I do not want to see an authoritarian society where old people rule young people. That's just as bad, I think.

—Could you comment on the way that we define young people, and the similarities with that and the way that we define older people? I see the same stereotypes toward young children that exist toward the elderly. We treat children as being more immature and irresponsible than they really are.

JL: Well, that's interesting because the only two groups that you can really abuse are animals and children. You are not supposed to abuse human adults. You can abuse children, but the average adult will call it spanking. It's all right to do that. Have you ever noticed that just before Thanksgiving we demean turkeys? About a week before Thanksgiving I see in the newspapers and on the radio and on television: "Those stupid, ugly birds. We are going to eat you." It's all right to eat an ugly, stupid bird. You are not supposed to eat a smart, beautiful bird, but it's all right to eat a turkey. Well, we do the same things with human beings. Just before we want to really discriminate against a group, we demean them. Just before we wanted to take land from the American Indians, just before we burned their villages, just before we wanted to take Texas from Mexico, just before we restricted jobs from the Chinese or the Japanese, when times were rough, all of a sudden, stereotypes became extremely negative. Suddenly, people become turkeys. They either become animals or they become little children. And it makes it all right to do all those nasty things. It seems that the primary function of prejudice is to justify discrimination.

BIBLIOGRAPHY

Fischer DH: *Growing Old in America*. New York, Oxford University Press, 1977.

Jacobs J: *Fun city: An Ethnographic Study of a Retirment Community*. New York, Holt, Rinehart, and Winston, 1974.

Levin J: *The Functions of Prejudice*. New York, Harper and Row, 1975.

Levin J, Levin WC: *Ageism: Prejudice and Discrimination Against the Elderly*. Belmont, Calif, Wadsworth, 1980.

Ryan W: *Blaming the Victim*. New York, Random House, 1971.

CHAPTER 17

The Helping Hand Strikes Again: Unintended Consequences of Child Abuse Reporting

Eli H. Newberger

Twenty years after the publication of the influential medical report, "The Battered Child Syndrome" (Kempe et al, 1962), it seems fitting to reflect on the significance and the effectiveness of the modern child protection movement. The Kempe paper stimulated an outpouring of editorial concern in professional and lay media. The United States Children's Bureau promulgated a model child abuse reporting law. By the late 1960s, all states had laws mandating the identification and reporting of abused children. Although the problem had been documented for as long as we have had records of mankind, and notwithstanding a century-old activism against cruelty to children in the United States, it is notable that it took a medical article and a recasting of child abuse as a medical syndrome to stimulate a broad national concern (Newberger and Bourne, 1978).

In retrospect, it is notable that this concern coincided with the civil rights movement of the 1960s, a time of activism for the rights of disadvantaged people, including children, a time when it was widely believed that state and national governments had not only the ability but the responsibility to provide, protect, and shelter where families could not.

By the early 1970s, substantial clinical literature and experience had accrued. It came to be generally understood in professional circles that people who abused children only rarely were cruel, sadistic murderers. They were troubled, burdened by psychological and family problems; and they could and should be helped, through treatment, to more adequately protect and to nurture their offspring (Steele and Pollock, 1974). Case report statistics suggested that by far the majority of the victims lived in poor families (Gil, 1978).

Service Idealism vs Civil Libertarianism

A humane philosophy of intervention evolved in the first decade after the publication of "The Battered Child Syndrome" article. Physical child abuse and its intervention were increasingly perceived to be associated with other human problems which could respond to an infusion of professional attention and personal good will and affection: child neglect, child sexual abuse, and deprivation of medical, educational, and moral supports for a child's growth.

In February 1971, a US Senate Subcommittee on Children and Youth was created. With no authority over existing programs, it became a forum for advancing proposals made at the 1970 White House Conference on Children. The need for a coherent federal role in the identification, prevention, and treatment of abused and neglected children stimulated the drafting of legislation. The discussion, and politics, which culminated in the signing of Public Law 93-247 in 1974 have been described clearly by Ellen Hoffman (1979), who served as Staff Director of this subcommittee. Among the points of conflict at the time were the extent to which resources should be committed to research or services, and the appropriate role of the federal government. In Ellen Hoffman's words:

> Another priority question revolved around whether the limited resources under the Act should be directed primarily at the children who are abused, children who are neglected, or both. The original Senate bill did not even define "abuse" and "neglect." It was felt to be unnecessary because the law was to be a program of services, research and the like, not a punitive or regulatory measure. Moreover, an attempt at a federal definition might work unnecessary hardship on states and localities, which already had widely varying definitions in their own lives. The House, however, did insert a definition that included not only physical but also mental injury.
>
> The authors of the bill had no illusions that it would service all of the families implicated by reports of abuse or neglect so widely defined. This was a political judgement based on the recognition that funds available for the new program would not be adequate to provide services even to those children and families already defined as needing them.
>
> Thus, although there is not statutory statement, the legislative history (testimony, committee reports, and floor statements) reflects the clear intent of Congress that priority be given to helping children who are the victims of physical abuse [pp 168-169.]

This may have been the intention, but many physicians and social workers in this field of practice and officials in the Children's Bureau appear to have construed the mandate for the National Center on Child Abuse and Neglect differently. When the time came to stipulate a definition of child abuse in state statutes as a condition for eligibility for the states' shares of federal funds, officials in the Department of Health, Education, and Welfare defined child abuse broadly, and they elaborated a long list of professionals to be mandated to report. This action was taken notwithstanding a growing concern among a different professional community that unless the flow of case reports into the child welfare service system were controlled, the system could be overwhelmed. This view was expressed, in fact, in the report of an expert commission to study child abuse reporting (Sussman and Cohen, 1975). The debate between the service idealists who would open wider the portals of entry in the service system, and the civil libertarians who were concerned with the prospect of more incompetent and damaging intrusions into family life, appears to have been resolved in favor of the idealists (Zigler, 1979).

Prevalence

At this time, no one could have foreseen that the prevalence of child abuse, however narrowly defined, was far greater than was believed at the time of the publication of the "Battered Child Syndrome" paper or the signing of Public Law 93-247. Where 7000 to 8000 reports were received nationally in 1967 and 1968, over 700,000 were received in 1978 (National Center on Child Abuse and Neglect, 1980). Estimates of severe inflicted injuries to children deriving not from case reports, but from household surveys, range from one to four million incidents per year (Gelles, 1978, Gil, 1970*).

Nor was it possible to predict that the humane and generous expansion of social programs during the administration of Lyndon Johnson would contract in the years since the national child abuse program was passed. I have no doubt that had professionals, like me, known then what we know now, we would never have urged on Congress, federal officials, and state legislators broadened concepts of child abuse as the basis for reporting legislation.

Help and Punishment

For we now see in every state a vexing and cruel dilemma. In many, if not most, jurisdictions, the only way to get social services such as day care, homemakers and counseling to children and parents is to make a child abuse or neglect case report. Child welfare services have, to a great degree, become protective services. Are they protecting children? Without

---

* Gil conducted a survey of a representative sample of American citizens in which respondents were asked whether they personally knew of incidents in which children were abused. The 95% confidence interval for the extrapolation to the country as a whole was 2.5 to 4 million incidents. Gelles surveyed 1146 two-parent families with at least one child between 3 and 17 in the home and asked, using the "Conflict Tactics Technique," direct questions about family violence. Between 1.4 and 1.9 million children were seen as vulnerable to physical injury; 3.6% of the parental respondents used violence which could have led to injury in the survey year.

question, in many cases they are. A higher level of awareness of child abuse and neglect among professionals, parents, and children, has led to the timely identification, and certainly the rescue, of many families in jeopardy.

But in order to help a family, a physician must, in effect, condemn the parents with a diagnosis that implicitly means that they are bad parents. Sometimes, the only resources available are hurtful. In many localities, children reported as victims of neglect or abuse are placed in foster home care as the first, rather than the last resort. There, ironically and tragically, they may languish for years, often shuttled from foster home to foster home, and their health and emotional needs are often cruelly neglected by the very system designated to serve them.

Or, perhaps more frequently, the reports are unattended, or are given only superficial screening and review. Then, children may suffer more grievous harms until their injuries may come to light in the criminal courts where their parents may be prosecuted.

This scandalous situation has resulted in several class-action law suits in which those initiated in Massachusetts by the Massachusetts Committee for Children and Youth and by Greater Boston Legal Services have recently led to court orders assuring a child's right to a timely investigation when she or he is the subject of a child abuse or neglect case report and specifying the maximum caseloads which protective service social workers can carry.

Ironically, the promise implicit in the child abuse reporting laws has become an empty promise for many children. This is all the more regretable in light of present knowledge about what we can do effectively to treat child abuse (Cohn, 1979).

The issues we face in this area of practice go beyond the acts and the consequences of reporting. They have to do also with some fundamental realities of the provision of medical care and social services.

Class and Racial Bias in Reporting

My colleague Robert Hampton and I are completing a study of hospital recognition and reporting of child abuse which documents the pervasive significance of *class* and *race* in the defining, identifying, and reporting of child abuse. (Hampton and Newberger, 1985). The findings are disturbing.

The study is a secondary analysis of the National Study of the Incidence and Severity of Child Abuse and Neglect of the National Center on Child Abuse and Neglect. The data were collected between May 1, 1979 and April 30, 1980. A careful effort was made to collect data on a sufficient number of subjects to permit an extrapolation to the national experience. Eight hundred and five cases of child abuse and neglect came to the attention of the hospitals in the study during the year of examination. A projected estimate of 77,380 cases of abuse and neglect suspected by hospital professionals was derived from this number by weighing and multiplying these reports, employing standard sampling methods. Strict criteria for inclusion in the national incidence measurement had been articulated, and 35,088 cases fell within the scope of these definitions. Compared to other agencies in the sample, hospitals identified children who were younger, had younger parents, and who contained relatively higher proportions of families in urban areas (65.8% vs 42.1%) and who were black (25% vs 16%). There were no major differences between the hospital and other agencies with respect to income, mode of medical payment (public or private), proportion of single parent families, sex of the child, and other demographic factors.

Nationally, approximately 652,000 children met the operational definitions of abuse and neglect during the study year, of whom 212,400 would have been known to the local child protective service agencies. Hospitals identified many more cases of physical abuse than did other agencies. The proportion of cases in this category alone exceeded the proportion of physical, sexual, and emotional abuse cases recognized by all the other agencies; over half the hospital cases were in one or another category of abuse.

The study was unique in its ability to measure which cases were selected for reporting. Never before had a systematic effort been made to identify cases before reports were made and to ascertain the differences between the cases which were reported and those which were not.

The ethnic and social class distributions for all children reported to child protection agencies as alleged victims of abuse or neglect were similar to the sample distribution, but there was significant *underreporting* of white and more affluent families. Surprisingly, notwithstanding the fact that hospitals indentify more serious cases of child abuse and neglect than other agencies, serious injuries are often unreported.

Although hospitals reported cases of abuse and neglect within the scope of the study definitions more frequently than did other agencies, they failed to report almost half of the cases which should have been reported.

Further analysis studied in detail the differences between reported and unreported cases. The following factors appeared to strongly affect case reporting: income, the role of the mother in maltreatment, emotional abuse, race, employment of the mother, sexual abuse, emotional neglect, the number of victims and the education of the mother. Disproportionate numbers of unreported cases were victims of emotional abuse in families of higher income, whose mothers were alleged to be responsible for the injuries, and who were white.

The data suggest that class and race, but not severity, define who does and who does not get reported by hospital personnel to child protection agencies.

They suggest that the reporting process contributes to the widespread mythology that these problems are confined to people who are poor or who are members of ethnic minorities. This myth, that families who abuse their children are different from the rest of us, has led this country to identify child abuse and neglect as "poor people's problems," for which we have created traditionally programs of poor quality; programs, which like the current national child protection program, may mete out punishment in the guise of help.

Criminalization

We now find a movement across the country to remedy the problems in the overburdened child protection agencies by making it required for professionals to report cases to police departments and to district attorneys. The failures in our ability to provide help to troubled individuals and families are, it would appear, being addressed by criminalizing family problems and, unfortunately, by demeaning those professional groups, especially social workers who are best able to provide help to abused and neglected children and their parents.

The data from our study suggest that were reports to be mandated to more intrusive and punitive agencies, even fewer white and more affluent families would be reported. Child abuse and neglect will appear even more to be the poor people's problems than we may want them to appear to be.

To make matters worse, the Department of Health and Human Services promulgated a regulation which required that incidents where severely handicapped infants were denied medical services to assure their survival must be reported on a tollfree number to a national clearing house or to local child protection agencies. Signs are to be posted in all nurseries to announce this policy. Hospitals which do not comply risk losing federal reimbursements for services, training, and research.

This policy imposes an inappropriate burden on agencies which are inadequately equipped to do what they are supposed to do, and which are manifestedly unprepared to investigate medical practices, parental suffering and grief, and hospital professional procedures. It represents a further extension of the notion that through the provision of child protective services, we police and control family life.

The child protection movement in this country is now at an important crossroads. We must decide whether our objective is, truly, as the laws state, to protect children and to strengthen families by offering help to them.

Reporting and Prevention

By its very nature, child abuse and neglect case reporting leads to intrusions into family life. This is necessary to assure the protection of thousands of children each year. My concern is that reporting as a way of getting services to families may no longer be an effective national policy to treat child abuse. Rather, we should consider the needs of all the children who might be vulnerable to maltreatment. Through a national program focused on prevention, addressed to every family, we should be able effectively to put to use our existing knowledge. (Newberger and Newberger, 1983; Newberger, Newberger and Hampton, 1983).

The essential question with regard to child abuse reporting is not whether to narrow the definitions; it is whether reporting is to be the method we choose to treat the problem. Reporting has not been a wholesale failure; but it has not been an unqualified success. Reporting of child abuse must now be supplanted by a marshaling of resources toward prevention, along with an effort to train, among others, physicians and medical workers more appropriately and wisely to make use of preventive and therapeutic resources.

BIBLIOGRAPHY

Cohn AH: Effective treatment of child abuse and neglect. *Social Work* 1979;24:513-519.

Gelles RJ: Violence towards children in the United States. *Am J Orthopsychiatry* 1978;48:580-592.

Gil DG: *Violence Against Children: Physical Child Abuse in the United States.* Cambridge, Harvard University Press, 1970.

Gil DG: Societal violence and violence in families, in Eekelaar JM, Katz SN (eds): *Family Violence.* Toronto, Butterworths, 1978.

Hampton RL, Newberger EH: Child abuse incidence and reporting by hospitals: Significance of severity, class, and race. *Am J Public Health* 1985;75:56-60.

Hoffman E: Policy and politics: the child abuse prevention and treatment act, in Bourne R, Newberger EH (eds): *Critical Perspectives on Child Abuse.* Lexington, DC Heath, 1979, pp 157-170.

Kempe CH, Silverman FN, Steele BF, et al: The battered child syndrome. *JAMA* 1962;181:17.

National Center on Child Abuse and Neglect: National analysis on official child neglect and abuse reporting (1978). U.S. Dept. of Health and Human Services. DHHS Publications (OHDS 80-30271), 1980.

Newberger EH, Bourne R: The medicalization and legalization of child abuse. *Am J Orthopsychiatry* 1978;48:593.

Newberger CM, Newberger EH: Prevention of child abuse: theory, myth, practice. *J Preventive Psychiatry* 1982;1:1-8.

Newberger EH, Newberger CM, Hampton RL: Child abuse: The current theory base and future research needs. *J Am Acad Child Psychiatry* 1983;22:262-268.

Steele BF, Pollock CB: A psychiatric study of parents who abuse infants and small children, in Helfer RE, Kempe CH (eds): *The Battered Child*, ed 2. Chicago, University of Chicago Press, 1974, pp 80-133.

Sussman A, Cohen SJ: *Reporting Child Abuse and Neglect: Guidelines for Legislation*. Cambridge, Ballinger, 1975.

Zigler E: Controlling child abuse in America: An effort doomed to failure? in Bourne R, Newberger EH (eds): *Critical Perspectives on Child Abuse*. Lexington, DC Heath, 1979, pp 171-213.

INDEX